HOLY
MOMENTS

HOLY MOMENTS

Robert T. Young

THE UPPER ROOM
Nashville, Tennessee

Scripture quotations not otherwise identified are from the Revised Standard Version of the Bible, copyrighted 1946, and © 1971 by the Division of Christian Education, National Council of the Churches of Christ in the United States of America, and are used by permission.

Scripture quotations designated KJV are from the authorized King James Version of the Bible.

Any scripture quotation designated AP is the author's paraphrase.

Excerpt from *You! Jonah!* by Thomas John Carlisle, copyright © 1968 by William B. Eerdmans Publishing Company, is reprinted by permission. *You! Jonah!* now available only from the author at 437 Lachenauer Drive, Watertown, NY 13601.

Excerpt from *Markings* by Dag Hammarskjöld, trans. by Leif Sjoberg and W. H. Auden, copyright © 1964 by Alfred A. Knopf, Inc. and Faber and Faber, Ltd., is reprinted by permission of the publisher.

Excerpt from *Notes on Love and Courage* by Hugh Prather, copyright © 1977 by Hugh Prather, is reprinted by permission of Doubleday & Co., Inc.

Selected lines from "I Am Lonely for Your Touch" appearing in *Lord, Could You Make It a Little Better?* by Robert A. Raines, copyright © 1972 by Word, Inc., are reprinted by permission of the author.

Selected lines from *Prayers* by Michel Quoist, trans. by Agnes M. Forsyth and Anne Marie de Commaille, copyright © 1963 by Sheed & Ward, Inc., are reprinted by permission of Andrews, McMeel & Parker. All rights reserved.

Selected lines by Carl Sandburg from "High Moments," copyright © 1960 by Carl Sandburg. Reprinted from his volume *Honey and Salt* by permission of Harcourt Brace Jovanovich, Inc.

"Spirit of the Living God" by Daniel Iverson, copyright 1935, 1963 by Moody Press, Moody Bible Institute of Chicago, is reprinted by permission.

Book Design: Harriette Bateman
First Printing: June, 1985 (3)
Second Printing: March, 1986 (3)
Third Printing: March, 1988 (3)
Library of Congress Catalog Card Number: 84–052229
ISBN: 0-8358-0513-1
Printed in the United States of America

Dedicated to

DR. CARLYLE MARNEY

friend, brother, healer, and fellow pilgrim
known to and loved by all as

"MARNEY"

Contents

Preface

Holy moments happen to us as God's spirit interacts with our spirits. Holy moments also happen to us as the lives and spirits of others reach out, touch, and reshape our lives and spirits. I want to express my thanks to God for persons whose lives have touched mine in beautiful and unforgettable ways in the conceiving, writing, and putting together of this book.

A friend once remarked to me, "It must be a lonely and awesome experience to write meditations or sermons. When you begin, it is just God and you and a blank piece of paper." It *is* awesome and lonely to write for reading or for preaching. As a rule, one begins with God, a blank piece of paper, and oneself. In this instance, I began also with a host of relationships and memories that unfolded as I worked through the holy moments I present here.

I want to express gratitude to the friends who have helped shape me and these writings. Thanks especially to my wife, Jackie; to our daughters and sons, Sherri, Terri, Rob, and Andrew; and to our son-in-law, Dean; they are in the midst of much of these writings. My thanks to Ann Kellam and Jackie Andrews, friends as well as secretaries at Duke University during my ministry there. My thanks to Betty Jean Britt and Mary Green, who typed and helped put these words in their final form at my present church, Broad Street United Methodist Church. A word of special gratitude is due to Peggy and Chandler Bryan who graciously allowed me to use their lakeside cottage for reflection and writing. I am grateful to those persons who graced the worship services at Duke University Chapel and here at Broad Street, those whose lives and influence lie behind and within many of these pages.

It has been a holy moment for me to reflect and write and share these holy moments. My wish is that some word here may help others to know and experience holy moments in their pilgrimages of life and faith in the days ahead.

HOLY
MOMENTS

1.

Holy Moments

Read Matthew 3:13–17.

*Jesus came from Galilee to the Jordan
to John, to be baptized by him.*
—Matthew 3:13

Our Lord experienced many holy moments in his life. Jesus' birth was a holy moment when God became one *of* us. Jesus' baptism was a holy moment when God became one *with* us. Jesus' death was a holy moment when God became one *for* us. Jesus' resurrection was a holy moment when God became one *to* us.

So, too, are our lives filled with holy moments: birth, death, and many life-changing moments in between. We have holy moments when we know life is sacred, purposeful, authentic, whole, and holy. We have holy moments when we know we have come from God, we return ultimately to God, and in the meantime, we belong to God. We are created in the image of God. We are persons conceived, formed, and birthed by God. We are living and breathing human beings who are children of the Almighty, our Father/Mother God, who is the Lord God everlasting. We never want to forget that!

Holy moments are bits of infinity when we

become aware of who we are: human, dependent, and in need; when we submit who we are to the grace of God; when we are blessed and we receive God's presence. This is what happened to Jesus at his baptism. He acknowledged his humanity. He submitted to baptism and received the grace of God. He heard God's voice and experienced God's presence and power.

After that, life was never the same for Jesus. From that moment on, he never looked back; he kept his hand to the plow. His relationships with his family, his friends, his hometown changed. His self-image changed. The way his neighbors saw him changed. His reputation changed.

A moment becomes holy for us when we see and are seen; we hear and are heard; we know life and feel alive; we seek and find; we ask and get answers; we reach and touch; we know and are known; we care and are cared about; we love and are loved. When life changes and we are never the same again, when we are able to say with Paul, "By the grace of God I am what I am" (1 Cor. 15:10), we know holy moments.

Holy moments seldom if ever just happen to us. They do not ordinarily just come upon us, without our taking the initiative, assuming some responsibility, making some decisions. That's what Jesus did. After thirty years, he decided it was time to make a move, to be serious about life, to make a commitment. He decided. He moved. He risked.

All of us live through holy moments, moments that are life-changing, unforgettable, freeing, fulfilling, and promising. *Kairos* moments is the Greek way to put it. Such moments are decisive, significant, and critical.

A moment. Just a moment. That seems to be such an infinitesimally small portion of time. It seems incredible but true that life is often created and re-created, made and remade, shaped and reshaped, focused and refocused in one, single, solitary moment of time.

All of us have holy moments to which we return to be nourished and sustained, to be guided and directed, to be named and renamed. These moments tell us who we are, to whom we belong, to what we have made commitments. Holy moments give us our sense of direction, our place, our relationship, our identity, our sense of belonging and fulfillment.

I still remember the impact of the first time my dad called me "son." I was plowing in the field (I think the only time I *ever* plowed on our small farm!), and Dad wanted me to do something right that I was doing wrong. I don't remember the correcting or the scolding. What I remember is that my dad called me "son." I go back to that every now and then. We all have holy moments to which we return.

Holy moments may be all the moments we have between life and death. Mary Jean Irion, in her book *Yes, World,* writes, "I have come from infinity and I go to infinity, between which events, for a little time, I came to celebrate that miracle which I could never fathom."

Just for a little time, a moment, to celebrate. "Just for a moment," Emily cries in Thornton Wilder's *Our Town.* "Oh, Mama, just look at me one minute as though you really saw me....Just for a moment...."

A moment, just a moment, truly can be holy. Theologian Henri Nouwen knows the significance of a moment as he writes in *The Wounded Healer,* "Love not only lasts forever, it needs only a second to come about."

Some moments seem to break us, at least for a time. I'm not sure these moments are all always holy, but we will surely have some moments when we fall or fail, are rejected, become incurably ill, know painful separation, see a loved one die, are confused, or are misunderstood.

Eugene Kennedy helps us see this in *The Heart of Loving* when he writes, "There can be a lifetime of pain in an intense moment of separation."

We also gain insight from Father Paneloux's words in Camus' book, *The Plague.* At first, Paneloux preaches that the epidemic in the town of Oran is God's judgment on a town that deserves it. Later, he watches a small child afflicted with the plague, and at the height of the child's agony Paneloux prays, "My God, spare this child!" The child is not spared, however. That experience changes the priest so that never again can he believe that eternal bliss will make up for the anguish and pain of any one child's innocent suffering. He asks, "Who would dare assert that eternal happiness can compensate for a single moment's human suffering?" Holy moments can include moments of pain and tragedy.

Thomas John Carlisle shows us the poignancy that trouble can bring in the poem "In Touch," from his book *You! Jonah!*:

Distress did it.
Not Easy Street.
Not Acrilon Avenue.
Not Prosperity Place
or Brightview Boulevard.
Nor Fair Haven
or the Bay of Serenity
or the Island of Tranquillity
but off-course winds
and the Straits of Adversity
and the tempests of disaster
that howled to Charybdis.
The deep was round about me.
Emergency exits were barred.
I was pitted against perdition.
In a ravenous cavity
I was swallowed up.
Better late than never
I remembered the Forgotten.
My troubles put me in touch.

Some holy moments of struggle put us in touch with the Forgotten One.

Some moments make us. I must claim that they are all holy moments, because they are the positive times when we are affirmed and accepted, know deep satisfaction, are reunited and reconciled, share communion, know triumph, experience new life, find and are found by a new friend, acquire new insights, discover new ideas, or make genuine commitments to God, to others, and to self.

In his book *Markings,* Dag Hammarskjöld has an entry dated Whitsunday, 1961:

I don't know Who—or what—put the question,
I don't know when it was put. I don't even

17

remember answering. But at some moment I did answer *Yes* to Someone—or Something—and from that hour I was certain that existence is meaningful and that, therefore, my life, in self-surrender, had a goal.

We all experience holy moments. Holy moments described by a word, a look, a note, a call, a decision, a meeting, a step, a gesture, a movement, a touch, a prayer. Holy moments come when who we are is confronted, threatened, questioned, confirmed, affirmed, claimed, named, and blessed. And it takes just a moment. Indeed, there are boundary moments, moments of moment, holy moments around us all the time.

Luke describes Jesus' baptism as a holy moment, "And when Jesus also had been baptized and was praying...the Holy Spirit descended upon him" (Luke 3:21–22). After he was baptized, Jesus was praying. That is worth our remembering. One way to know more holy moments is by praying as Jesus did.

Recently I began to set aside a half hour every morning for prayer. I pray for others, the world, the church, and myself. This prayer-time has made a noticeable difference in my spiritual and personal life. Not that all of my moments are now holy. Not by any means. There are *some* holy moments now; there are *more* than I used to have.

Perhaps we all need to find some new time to pray, to open ourselves more and more to the love, the grace, and the presence of God as did our Lord. All our moments won't be holy, but in prayer, we will begin to know some new and lasting holy moments like we've never known before.

The beauty of holy moments in and through prayer is shared by Hugh Prather in his book *Notes on Love and Courage*:

> The talking does something. I pray to God, my friend, and it changes me, if only for a moment. I feel myself siding with what is good in me. I feel cleansed, and I look around with more gentleness. Relationships appear to re-form on a new basis: the gentleness in me seeing the gentleness in others. I sense my own beauty and health, and I see a core of goodness in others. The world dances for a moment.

God knows that with all the war and threats of war and enmity and brokenness around us it would be, oh, so beautiful if the world could dance, even for a moment, a holy moment.

Questions for Reflection or Discussion

1. What are some things that make a moment, or an experience, holy for you? What happens? What or who is present?
2. Some holy moments make us; some try us. Reflect upon a holy moment that helped make you. Reflect upon a holy moment that tried you. How do you feel now about those that made you and about those that tried you?
3. Reflect upon, and share with another, a *kairos,* a life-changing holy moment you have had.
4. Recall some holy moment in various experiences in the Bible. Can you identify with the main character in some of them? For example, Moses before the burning bush, David being confronted

by Nathan the Prophet, Jonah running from God, Simeon at the time the child Jesus was brought to him, Peter being called "Satan" by Jesus, the woman of the city pouring ointment on Jesus' feet and being forgiven. There are many others. Think on these and share your feelings about how you see yourself in them.

5. Can a holy moment happen between you and another person? What makes that experience holy? Does something "spiritual" have to be felt for the moment to be holy?

2.

Christmas

Read Luke 3:2b–6.

> *All flesh shall see the salvation of God.*
> —Luke 3:6

Christmas is a holy time, a holy moment for God's people. Few words in the English language elicit such deep and varied responses as does the word *Christmas*. When we talk about Christmas, when we think about Christmas, we are touched in ways that we cannot control. Just for a moment, think about Christmas and let your thoughts and feelings come to the surface.

In the United States, we surely have enough time to think about Christmas. The commercial side of Christmas comes at us as soon as Halloween decorations are removed from stores. For two months, Christmas advertisements come our way. For one month in the church, we anticipate Christmas as we observe Advent, the time of preparation for Christ's birth. Christmas brings out all kinds of responses in us.

We feel many contradictions. Christmas calls us to believe and reminds us of our unbelief; calls us to faith and reminds us of our faithlessness; calls us to follow and reminds us of how reluctant we are to respond to God's claim on us. Christmas speaks of peace but we're surrounded by violence; tells of joy but we see sadness all around; is for singing but the last thing we feel like doing is singing; brings us hope but we feel much despair; talks of presence but we feel all alone; reminds us of love but we seem in the midst of sheer selfishness; is the story of salvation but we see a world bent on self-destruction.

Christmas stirs our spirits in ways no other season, no other holiday does. We say, "Christmas," and we visualize unforgettable pictures: the adoration of the Magi; a winter's snow; the Holy Family; Christmas trees; candlelight services.

At the mention of Christmas, we recall words and phrases: "Unto you is born...a Savior"; *holy; angels;* "O Little Town of Bethlehem..."; *shepherds; gifts; love; star;* "The Word became flesh"; "My soul doth magnify the Lord"; *Incarnation;* "You shall call his name Jesus, for he will save his people from their sins"; *Mary; "Gloria in excelsis Deo."*

Christmas makes us think of places that are special to us: home; church; kitchen; altar; stable.

People who are special to us come to mind: mother, father, husband, wife, children, neighbors we love, friends who love us, teachers who have helped us, boyfriend, girlfriend, grandmother, grandfather, aunt, uncle, cousins, preacher, grocer, mail carrier. Christmas is a moment, a holy moment, when lives that have blessed us come back vividly to bless us again.

Christmas is what T. S. Eliot describes in his poem "Burnt Norton" as "the still point of the turning world"... "where past and future are gathered." There is no other moment that so beautifully, so painfully, and so lastingly gathers past, present, and future for us as does Christmas!

But many of us are like the person who commented two weeks before Christmas, "I'll be so glad when Christmas is here and gone. I wish it were over with already!" Christmas is *that* kind of experience for some of us, something to "get over with," to get behind us, simply to get through. For some of us, Christmas does not last very long; it comes and goes quickly, like a Roman candle on the Fourth of July, like a shooting star flaming across the sky, or like the first snowflakes of early winter. For some of us, Christmas is very short-lived. It comes. It goes. It is over. That's it. No mark on us. No change for us.

The good news of Christmas is never over. The Word is always present. The greatest gift this world has ever received is still with us—that is the holy moment of Christmas. That means that God cares for us, God has made the son known to us, for unto us a child is born, unto us a son is given, and his name shall be called "Wonderful Counselor, Mighty God, Everlasting Father, Prince of Peace" (Isa. 9:6, AP). We can know that today. We don't want Christmas to be a shooting star or a melting snowflake. We want Christmas to last and last and last, in all the beautiful, warm, pain-filled, hope-filled ways that it possibly can.

God tells us that Christmas is special, Christmas is different, Christmas is for us, Christmas is God's time, Christmas is holy. Christmas can last!

Christmas is that time when little seems big and

big seems little, when close is far and far is very close, when the distant is home and home is everywhere, when the old become as children and all children become wise, when woman is at her greatest and man at his humblest. Christmas is that time when the very best in us comes out, when we are most tender and most vulnerable, when we are most loving and most sensitive, when we hurt the deepest and feel with all our senses, when we feel most alone and most in family, when we feel most distant and most intimate.

Christmas is that holy time that is for all of us both fact and fantasy, real and imagined, historic and created, concretion and illusion. It is as local as one family and as inclusive as God's whole earth. It is more than Israel hoped for, expected, or could comprehend. Christmas is more than we can hope for, understand, or describe.

Christmas is that holy story that tells of the greatest of kings, the simplest of babies; that tells about a time when shepherds are wise, when rulers bow down, when the wise seem foolish, and when the simple know all there is to know.

Paul was surely correct when he wrote:

> God chose what is foolish in the world to shame the wise, God chose what is weak in the world to shame the strong, God chose what is low and despised in the world . . . to bring to nothing things that are, so that no human being might boast in the presence of God. [God] is the source of your life in Christ Jesus, whom God made our wisdom, our righteousness . . . and redemption.
>
> —1 Corinthians 1:27–30

Christmas confuses the wisdom of the wise and confounds the logic of the philosophers. But what is that to those who know of Christmas? For Christmas speaks the message of the heart, sings the song of the soul, and thrills the wellsprings of the spirit.

Christmas expresses the hope that the world as it is, is not the world as it is to be. Christmas is a time when God says, ''This is for you.'' We reply, ''For us?'' God responds, ''Yes, for you! For everybody!''

And then, we are brought up short by the realities of our world and we ask ourselves, *How can we possibly celebrate Christmas in a time like this, in a world such as ours, in the midst of a world bent on going its own way and not God's way? How can we even think of celebrating?*

Celebrating Christmas in a world like this is like eating a banquet in the midst of a trash dump; like wearing soft, warm clothes in a freezing, wintry blizzard; like thinking rationally in the New Year's mob scene at Times Square; like hearing Handel's *Messiah* in the midst of the clanging commercial sounds of Christmas; like being sure of life and living, in the midst of pain, despair, and a foggy future; like sensing peace, knowing peace, feeling peace when turmoil and tension are all around.

Christmas in a world, in a day, in a time like this? It means to sing in the storm, smile in the rain, hold on in the gale, touch in the dark, see in the darkest of night. Celebrate Christmas in a time like this? Why that may very well be the only thing that does make sense; the only thing that touches us, that changes us, that lasts.

Celebrate Christmas? Make Christmas last? Not

the Christmas of jangled nerves, crowded shops, noisy streets, pushy grocery store crowds, post office lines, and Christmas card lists. Not the Christmas of "midnight specials on Friday afternoon"; not the Christmas of seductive perfume commercials; and not the Christmas of deceptively intoxicating alcohol ads and so-called Christmas parties. Not the kind of Christmas that we all want to be over and done with. That is not the Christmas we want to last.

"Oh, if Christmas could only last," I say when I hear, "For to you is born this day in the city of David a Savior, who is Christ the Lord" (Luke 2:11). I believe that "to you" means to you and to me! That's the Christmas I want to last.

Or when I hear, "They . . . found Mary and Joseph, and the babe lying in a manger" (Luke 2:16); and " 'This thing that has happened, which the Lord has made known to us' " (Luke 2:15); and "Mary kept all these things, pondering them in her heart" (Luke 2:19). I know that "this thing that has happened" is for you and me! That's the Christmas I want to last.

Or when I read how aged Simeon cried out after seeing the child Jesus, "Lord, now lettest thou thy servant depart in peace . . . for mine eyes have seen thy salvation" (Luke 2:29–30). I know that the salvation of God has come to you and to me! That's the Christmas I want to last.

Christmas does last when we remember the visit of the shepherds. They were drawn from their hills, where they were tending their sheep, to follow the voices of the angels and the stirring of God's spirit, to find the wee baby Jesus wrapped in swaddling cloths as they were told. In this holy moment, coming face-to-face with the fullness of God in human flesh, being overcome by the goodness of God they found in this unforgettable scene, they "returned, glorifying and praising God for all they had heard and seen" (Luke 2:20).

Christmas is a holy moment, which is why it is holy for all of us who let Christ come to us. God-in-Christ is my light and my salvation. Something happens in me, something happens to me, when I surrender to this God-in-Christ of Christmas.

Christmas gives me a word of hope, an experience of new life, and a new lift in my soul. That Christmas comes anytime.

Christmas gives me a song to sing, a cause to rejoice, a reason to lift up, look, and live. That Christmas comes anytime.

Christmas gives me a sense of the transcendent, of Someone beyond me, of Someone near and with me. I know, all over again, that God has come, is come, and will come. That Christmas comes anytime.

Christmas tells me I am loved, without any condition or qualification. I am loved in spite of my sin, in spite of my failures and weaknesses. I am loved because God loves us one and all. Helmut Thielecke says in *Being a Christian When the Chips Are Down* that the "meaning of Christmas is not in befogging the mind but in comforting the heart that knows it is lost." Without Christmas, without Christ, I know I am lost. With Christ, with Christmas, I know I am loved. Christmas also tells me I am to love; Christmas tells me I can love. Yes, I am loved and I can love without embarassment because of Christmas.

These are some of the things I need that Christmas brings. And, though I need these things all year long, I find them most at Christmas. This time around, I hope Christmas will last and last forever. This time around, I hope and pray that the holy moment of Christmas will last and last forever for you and for me.

Questions for Reflection or Discussion

1. Close your eyes, sit quietly for two or three minutes, and reflect upon the word *Christmas*. What are some images or sounds you experience? Talk about what some of these mean to you.

2. Is it okay near or at Christmas to have ambivalent, contradictory feelings, such as sadness and joy, singing and heavyheartedness, closeness and loneliness? How can we deal positively with our negative and destructive feelings at Christmas?

3. How was/is Christmas a turning point for all humankind? For the church? For you personally?

4. If you and your family or friends were to celebrate Christmas in the manner most in keeping with your own desires and needs, and in keeping with the Christian tradition, what are some things you would do?

5. Reflect upon what the message of Christmas means to you. Share some of that with another person (the group).

3.

Beginning/Ending

Read Genesis 1:1–31.

In the beginning God created the
heavens and the earth.

—Genesis 1:1

The psalmist writes, ''This is the day which the Lord has made; let us rejoice and be glad in it'' (Psalm 118:24). Is this a beginning or an ending?

Jesus spoke to his disciples, ''A little while, and you will see me no more; again a little while, and you will see me'' (John 16:16). Is this a beginning or an ending?

John in Revelation writes to the early church, ''Then I saw a new heaven and a new earth; for the first heaven and the first earth had passed away.... And he who sat upon the throne said, 'Behold, I make all things new' '' (Rev. 21:1, 5). Is this a beginning or an ending?

Life is full of beginnings and endings for all of us. The time of graduation comes and goes for our high school and college students. Is this a beginning or an ending? Cold and snow end; warmth and rain begin. Winter ends; spring begins. Life is a series of transitions: ending/beginning, beginning/ending. Some of it we like; some of it we dislike. As a friend of mine said recently, "We are people who do not care much for endings. We are people of beginnings. We celebrate beginnings but want to forget endings." And we do.

The truth is that only as one experience comes to an end can we begin another; the grace of God is present at the ending and at the beginning for any of us anytime. No matter where we are in our individual pilgrimages at this moment in life, God can give us a new beginning.

This message must be important for us to know because it runs like a golden thread through the Old Testament, the New Testament, history, the life of the church, and our experiences. Beginning and ending, that's what life is all about.

We celebrate beginnings but want to forget endings. We do want to forget endings. We don't like to have a door closed in our face, or watch a good movie end, or see the curtain fall on a good play. We don't like to come to the last page of a good book, or see the last leaf fall, or drink the last drop of a good cold drink. We don't like to spend our last dollar, or run out of ink, or see darkness come. We don't like to see death come to a loved one. We'd much rather shake hands in greeting than in parting. We don't like to kiss good-bye. We don't care much for endings.

We do celebrate beginnings. Christmas, the beginning of the life of Jesus the Christ. Memorial Day, celebrating the beginning of peace at the end of war. July 4, the beginning of a new country. Easter, the beginning of a new faith, a new people, a new church. New Year's Day, the beginning of new hopes and aspirations. Birth, the beginning of new life and promise. Engagement for a couple in love, new commitments and new tomorrows. A new friend, the beginning of a new life for both of you. Graduation and commencement, a time to commence anew, truly a new beginning. A new job, new responsibilities and new opportunities for you and others. A wedding, a time to celebrate a deep new beginning. We want to forget endings but we celebrate beginnings.

The only real problem with that, however, is that one is never quite sure when an experience is an ending or when it is a beginning. Could it be that it really does not matter, because at the ending and at the beginning the grace of God is always present?

We see that in scripture. The Old Testament begins, ''In the beginning God created'' (Gen. 1:1). Noah celebrated a new beginning at the end of the Flood. The Exodus for Moses and his people began when captivity ended. At the end of Jacob's wrestling with the angel, a new life began. At the end of his running as far and as long as he could, Jonah began anew. Amos was called to end work in the fields and begin his preaching for God.

In the New Testament Mark's first words are, ''The beginning of the gospel of Jesus Christ'' (1:1). Remember Peter? On one occasion, he must have felt he was at the end. Jesus said to him, ''Get behind me, Satan!'' (Matt. 16:23). That was the ending, which made possible the beginning, when Jesus said to him, ''You are Peter, and on this rock I will build my church'' (Matt. 16:18).

Jesus spoke of new beginnings: ''Unless you . . .

become like children'' (Matt. 18:3); ''You must be born anew'' (John 3:7); ''Do this . . . in remembrance of me'' (1 Cor. 11:25).

Surely, the most dramatic and most powerful beginning at the ending, the one that changed the world for all time and revealed to us God's eternal plan, is seen in the life, death, and resurrection of Christ. This is a new beginning for Christ's holy church.

Jesus was condemned and beaten, ordered to be crucified. He was jeered, spat upon, mocked, and forced to carry his own cross. He traveled the *Via Dolorosa,* the Way of Sorrows, all alone. At Golgotha, only four of his followers stood by him, three women, one man. On that ''place of the skull,'' the soldiers had orders to carry out. They were good soldiers; they did their duty, effectively and completely.

Jesus died. And when darkness came on that awe-full Friday, two words described the scene: *the end!* But, thank God, God has the final and ongoing word. As John Claypool powerfully puts it in his book *Tracks of a Fellow Struggler,* written about the struggle with and death from leukemia of his eleven-year-old daughter, ''The point is, life never comes to a complete dead end.'' We all know the story. Jesus' crucifixion was the end. But then, the fullness of God's grace came rolling in, and it became the end which made possible the beginning.

Jesus had to go away, and the end had to come so that he could come again and the new beginning, life in the Spirit, could take place. Jesus said to his disciples, ''It is for your own good that I am going, because unless I go, the Comforter will not come to you; . . . but when the Spirit of truth comes, the Spirit will lead you'' (John 16:7, 13, AP). Thus, in Christ's absence a new and more intimate presence became possible, a presence that nurtured and sustained in the midst of tribulation.

The great mystery of the divine revelation is that God entered into intimacy with us not only by Christ's coming, but also by his leaving. Indeed, it is in Christ's absence, his ending, that an intimacy with him is so profound that we are able to experience new beginnings and say that Christ dwells with us and in us, and say that he is our food and drink and the center of our lives. Bonhoeffer was absolutely right when he wrote that the God who is with us is the God who forsakes us. Before God and with God we live without God. Only in Jesus' absence do we know the power and grace of Christ's presence.

John Wesley, at Aldersgate in May of 1738, after he had been reared in the Church of England and had preached for many years, began anew when he wrote in his journal, ''I felt my heart strangely warmed. . . . I did trust in Christ, Christ alone for salvation.'' A noted British writer, at the turn of the present century, said to a preacher friend, ''I've had enough of your doubts; tell me of your affirmations.'' Give me a new beginning.

The new beginning means new life and hope and promise for us. This is when we speak a new language, sing a new song, have a new image of self, value other brothers and sisters in a new way, perceive and act on life-and-death issues with new and bold convictions. This is when we become a new creation, have new life, and are new persons in Christ Jesus our Lord.

The ending which makes possible the beginning. You've been there, perhaps many times. The loss of a loved one is an ending but also the beginning of a new and different way of life without someone very dear. A serious illness may seem to be an ending, with the pain and despair, fear and anxiety it brings, but then new life and a new outlook on life, health, family, and friends may follow. Graduation time, a time of ending friendships and facing the unknown, makes possible new beginnings of life, vocation, and commitment.

Carlyle Marney once shared an unforgettable story with some of us. He said a physician friend of his had treated a young woman patient all her life. She was confined to a wheelchair and had never walked a step. One day, as the doctor was examining her, he said, "You know, Elizabeth, with all the pain and suffering you've gone through, I guess sometimes you wish you had never been born, don't you."

The doctor said her face sparkled and her eyes lit up, and she replied, "I wouldn't have missed it for the world."

"I wouldn't have missed it for the world."

We've been there. The ending which makes possible the beginning! The ending or many endings in life which may cause others to look at us and wonder if we wish we had never been born. In those moments, our hearts are warmed, our eyes sparkle, and deep in our soul, in spite of pain, death, and hurt we exclaim, "We wouldn't have missed it for the world!"

And so it is that the ending of one experience makes possible the beginning of a new. Surgery has to end before healing can begin. Dating has to end before marriage can begin. As Jesus reminds us, the pains of labor have to end before birth occurs. War has to end before peace can begin. Hatred has to end before harmony can begin. The great affirmations of the Christian faith tell us that dawn follows the midnight, daylight follows the darkness, and life follows death.

I'm told it is a breathtaking experience to go through the Endless Caverns in Virginia. Visitors go from room to room to view the stalactites and stalagmites formed uniquely underground. When visitors come to the last room, the guide has everyone stand against the wall. The lights are dimmed and then turned off entirely. Then begins the gradual lighting of the formations above a pool of water. The picture is like looking upon jewels hanging above a miniature lake with the dawn breaking upon them. It provides a beautiful ending to a memorable experience.

The guide then says, "This is not the end of the caverns. This is just as far as we go. Our explorers have gone many, many miles beyond this point. They have discovered larger rooms than any you have passed through and looked upon more beautiful sights than any you have seen. This is not the end. This is just as far as we go today. That is why we call them the Endless Caverns."

Life, for you and me, is an endless chain of

experiences. This moment or experience is not the end. This is just as far as we have gone for the moment. This is the ending we know. And these endings make possible ever-new beginnings. Surely, in Christ, there are larger experiences, greater meanings, more beautiful moments than any we have passed through thus far.

A story is told of one of the leaders of the Protestant reformation, who, at a point when all was in turmoil for him, was asked where he would be when the princes and the people, the church and the state, all turned against him, when the end came for him and his movement. The answer he flashed back was sure and certain, "Where shall I be then? Why, then, as now, in the hands of almighty God."

God doesn't ask us if we are at the ending or the beginning. Our Lord says to us, "Lo, I am with you always" (Matt. 28:20).

Only as one experience is ending can we begin another. The grace of God is present at the end and at the beginning. Then, as now, we are always in the hands of almighty God.

God is able always to transform what come to us as endings and make of them glorious new beginnings, through the presence and power of Jesus Christ our Lord. Thanks be to God.

Questions for Reflection or Discussion

1. How do you feel about endings? About beginnings? Describe a recent ending experience and a recent beginning experience you have had.

2. How do we know, when do we know, that an experience is a beginning or an ending?

3. Would we have the Christian church today if Jesus had not experienced an "ending"? What do you think would have happened, as a result of Jesus' teaching and ministry, if he had not been crucified and then raised from the dead?

4. Can you recall some experience that you and others thought was an ending that really became a beginning? Talk about the movement of your feelings through that experience and through your changing your view about it.

5. Are there ways in which we can know that God's grace is present in a beginning or an ending experience?

6. How would you put some substance to the statement, "God's grace is present, at the ending and at the beginning"?

4.

Now

Read Matthew 25:1–13.

> *Those who were ready went in with him.*
>
> —Matthew 25:10

In the Gospel of Matthew (25:1–13), the parable about five wise and five foolish maidens is a lovely story with a dreadful ending. Five maidens were ready; five were not. Five came into the wedding feast; five were shut out because they had not known when the bridegroom was coming. He came at midnight and caught them all by surprise. Those who were prepared were saved. Those who were not prepared were locked out and lost. Therefore, all of us had better be ready, be prepared, because we know not when the Lord will come. And, if we don't want to get closed out, we'd better be ready every moment.

Paul writes in 2 Corinthians 6:2, "*Now* is the acceptable time... *Now* is the day of salvation" (italics added). Sure it is. Everyone knows that. Now...today...this very moment. When I was young, I heard these passages interpreted, "You must be ready *now*, this hour, this moment, because tomorrow may be too late! Be saved, for tomorrow may be too late!'' What do these words have to do with us today with all that's going on with us, around us, and in us just now?

It is important to reflect occasionally on how we can know life, real life in the here and now, not life after death or the grave. It is helpful to think about the holy moments we can know in the present moment of the now—to be ready to live with renewed interest and commitment and determination, in the here, the now, the present moment. We want to reflect some on the holiness of the now. If there were no present moment, there would be no holy moments, no now, no life for us. Except for the now, there would be no life, and there is only life.

Therefore, if being ready is good for when the bridegroom comes, then being ready is good for now. If now is the day of salvation, then now is a holy moment, not because tomorrow may be too late, but because this is what God desires for each of us—to know the holiness and goodness of the now.

We are to be ready now, not because the Lord will come and we may not be ready, not because the Lord may come unexpectedly, and not because the Lord may come at midnight and find us sleeping. We are to be ready now, because that is life. We are to be saved now, not because tomorrow may be too late, but because being saved means being whole, authentic, and integrated. It means being the child of God each of us is created, redeemed, and called to be in the here and now.

I believe that God was in the beginning—for now. I believe that God created—for now. I believe that Christ came, lived, cared, died, was raised—for now. I believe that the Holy Spirit is alive, active, and well—for now. As we read the New Testament, we are made aware that Jesus came to bring life and to bring it now.

Jesus did not tell the woman at the well she could find good water sometime in the future. He gave her water to quench her thirst forever in the now of that very moment. Jesus did not tell the woman taken in adultery that she would know forgiveness and be whole one day soon. No, he said, ''Your sins are forgiven,'' in the now. He did not tell the thief on the cross to be ready for his return when he comes again. No, Jesus said, ''This day,'' in the now.

Do you need forgiveness now? Are you thirsty now? Do you need to be made whole now? Are you searching for life now? Jesus did not say, ''I have come that you might have life and have it someday!'' No! He said, ''I have come that you might have life and have it abundantly'' (John 10:10, AP). The eternal is now; the kingdom is now.

So the word comes to us: Do not live in the past. Do not live in the tomorrow. Live fully in the now.

Let's think for a minute about the holy moment of the now, the glory of the now where we know life—not yesterday, not tomorrow, not fantasy, but reality. The glory of the now is that the now may be very simple and very ordinary. The now may be filled with fear or doubt or question, but that's okay. That is the way any now may be for any of us. That is the way it is in this now for you and me.

Dr. Wallace Fowlie, in his book *Journal of*

Rehearsals, has some meaningful words for us. To live in the now means

> to learn to live deeply within oneself. It means contemplating and understanding your own life, no matter how limited and monotonous and prosaic it seems to have been. It means reading a book, not for pleasure in the ordinary sense, but for learning more about mankind outside of your own life and in a language that enobles the human spirit. It means grateful for every pain in your body, for every lack in your life, for every bruise a friend or a foe gives you, for every heartache and every disappointment in love.

The glory of the now, in faith and in life, is that it is unpredictable. The now gives ambiguity rather than serenity, and it raises more questions than it answers. The now explores options rather than closure, affirms diversity rather than uniformity. It is often scary and not secure. The now is always searching and struggling rather than arriving and settling. The glory of the now means to live neither in a romanticized yesterday nor in an illusory tomorrow. It means to live in a tough, tiring, tense, and troublesome today, where our stomachs get tied in knots, our heads ache from front to back, where we hurt others and others hurt us. The glory of the now is that this is where life is hard. Life is very, very hard and very, very real.

All of this is why Jesus came—to make the now a holy-moment experience for each one of us. In his poem *I Am Lonely for Your Touch,* Robert A. Raines tells us that it is in the now that God will

sit with [us] by the bedside
walk with [us] by the roadside
stand with [us] by the graveside
pray with [us] and for [us]
    in every moment's need
let [us] be wise but not cynical
    innocent but not foolish
    strong but not callous
    weak but not despairing
give depth to [our] speech
    and significance to [our] action.

In the poem "For the Time Being" in *Collected Longer Poems* by W. H. Auden, the three Magi tell about this holy moment. The now is to help us "discover and know how to be truthful" . . . "how to be living" . . . "how to be loving" . . . "how to be human now." How to be holy now, how to be real now, how to be a child of God now.

Questions for Reflection or Discussion

1. How can we help others and ourselves to realize the real value and significance of the *now* moment?

2. Paul writes, "Now is the day of salvation." What does this mean? In what way(s) is this true for you?

3. Why do you believe Jesus constantly told his listeners, and thus tells us, "Watch! Be ready!"

4. If the now gives ambiguity rather than serenity, and raises more questions than it answers, what makes the now a holy moment?

5. Can it really be true that all of creation and all of

history and all of God's actions have been and are just to make it possible for you to experience the now moment? Can you believe you are of that much value to God? Is any one human being, or are all of us together, worth that much in God's sight?

5.

Covenant

Read 1 Peter 2:4–10.

*Once you were no people but now you
are God's people.*

—1 Peter 2:10a

Beginnings often bring holy moments to us. It is good to have new beginnings when we lay aside what has been, wipe the slate clean of the old and worn, and start over by putting the past behind us. Consider what new beginnings can mean for us: new relationships; new experiences; new ideas; new ways; new challenges; new decisions; new opportunities; new freedoms.

Beginnings can also be times to think about holy-moment covenants we can make with God, with others, or with self.

If we reflect about covenant in the biblical sense, we can understand some of the beauty of this holy moment. A covenant relationship with God is one we are free to enter, free to continue, and also free to leave. In covenant encounters in the Bible, God is the initiator, the primary actor, the motivator, the mover, the One who comes to us. Covenant with God means basically that we are privileged to receive and benefit from God's acts and that we are invited to join with

God in caring for others and for the world. Covenant consists of God's act and our response, and this is holy.

The call for us to relate in covenant with God goes back to creation itself: "In the image of God...male and female he created them" (Gen. 1:27). We are created in the image of God. This likeness with God is seen in the life and experiences of Noah, Moses, Abraham, Isaiah, Jeremiah, Jesus, the disciples, the early church.

Covenanting with God means many things. It means we are chosen, claimed, called, committed. It means we participate in and partake of commonality, community, communion. In covenant, God makes promises to us. God assumes responsibility and provides for us on the way of our pilgrimages; God gives us signs and symbols and sustenance along the way.

The call to covenant does not always come when we want it to come; it certainly did not come when Moses wanted it. It does not always come when we are ready; it did not for Jeremiah. It is not always what we expect or want; it certainly was not what Noah expected. God's call to us to enter into covenant does not always lead to success or victory or to our coming out ahead in the world's definition of these words. Covenant does not take us immediately into the promised land.

Michel Quoist writes in his book *Prayers*:

Lord, you seized me, and I could not resist you.
I ran for a long time, but you followed me.
I took bypaths, but you knew them.
You overtook me.
I struggled,

You won.
Here I am, Lord, out of breath, no fight left in
   me, and I've said "Yes" almost unwillingly.
When I stood there trembling like one defeated
   before his captor,
Your look of love fell on me.

The die is cast, Lord; I can no longer forget
   you. . . .
For I recognized you without seeing you.
I felt you without touching you,
I understood you without hearing you.
Marked by the fire of your love, I can no longer
   forget you.

It is high risk to wait upon God, to listen to the
word of God, to respond to the voice of God, to enter
into covenant with God. These are among the holiest
of holy moments.

It may mean, as it did for Noah, that it will rain
on us for forty days and forty nights. It may mean that
we will meander, as did Abraham, for many years in
the desert headed toward Canaan. It may mean, as it
did for the people of Israel, wandering for forty years
in the wilderness before reaching the Promised Land.
It may mean, as it did for our Lord after his baptism,
spending forty days and forty nights with the wild
beasts.

We have some strange notions about what
covenanting with God means for us. We seem to
believe that covenant with God is what *we* do, but it
is not. Covenant is what God has done, is doing, and
will do in us, with us, for us, and to us. We are the
ones who respond. We seem to believe that covenant
means deliverance, and we act as if it means deliver-

ance now, at this very moment. We think it means immediate deliverance from bondage to freedom, from guilt to forgiveness, from oppression to release.

Learning that that is not so has been very helpful to me in studying the Bible and in trying to understand God's dealings with our forebears in the faith. Somehow or other, I had the notion that if one were "saved," if one "only believed," if one "simply trusted in God," if one "responded to God's call," if one "entered into covenant with God," one immediately was delivered, made whole, released, freed, set upon dry land. Somehow, if one simply responded and said, "Yes, I believe. I trust in God. I accept God's love and grace. I will be faithful and obedient and responsible," then God would take one at once into the promised land.

This is the way it was with me. I had heard and felt God speak and call and come to me. I had tried, as best as I could, to respond and be faithful, obedient, loving, and caring. Yet I certainly was not in the promised land. I was still wandering in the desert. I was still filled with questions, doubts, uncertainties, and ambiguities. Life seemed to make little sense. There are still things I do not understand or know or see clearly. I am not yet in the promised land.

Most of us have had that feeling. We think we've heard and felt a word from God. We've tried to respond and obey. Yet we feel we're still not in the promised land. With feelings like this, there is an encouraging word for us: that is okay. That is the way covenant and life and faith, that is the way living and believing, really are.

As we read in the Old Testament and in the New

Testament about the covenanting experiences of God with Noah, Moses, Abraham, Isaiah, Jeremiah, Jesus, and the early church, we read of no experiences where the people of God move immediately through covenant from wilderness to promised land. Between covenant and the promised land, there is always wilderness, for Noah and his family; for Moses and the children of Israel; for Jesus and the disciples; for you and me. We have the notion that covenant with God is ours to control. Not at all. God is in control. The call, the claim, and the covenant often come to us in ways over which we have absolutely no control.

In the New Testament there are three covenanting or receiving images: baptism; the Lord's Supper; the Holy Spirit. It is easy to see how we might get the idea that we are greatly in control. It is evident in the way we express ourselves about these three images. We think baptism is something we *do*. We think the Lord's Supper is something we *take*. We think we *have* the Holy Spirit. These are very possessive, controlling verbs: *to do, to take, to have*.

Baptism is not something we do. It is something we *receive*. The Lord's Supper is not something we take. It is something we *receive*. We do not have the Holy Spirit. We *receive* the Holy Spirit. And each of these is a holy moment for us.

Covenant affirms who God is, who each of us is, and who all of us are together. Covenant means, "I will be your God . . . you shall be my people" (Jer. 31:33, AP), unconditionally, obediently, faithfully.

But that is risky business for all of us. The words from some of the hymns we coolly and often casually sing betray the high risk involved:

Breathe on me, Breath of God,
Fill me with life anew,
That I may love what thou dost love,
And do what thou wouldst do.
                              —Edwin Hatch

Have thine own way, Lord!
   Have thine own way!
Thou art the potter; I am the clay.
Mold me and make me after thy will,
While I am waiting, yielded and still.
                      —Adelaide A. Pollard

Spirit of the living God, fall afresh on me.
Spirit of the living God, fall afresh on me.
Melt me. Mold me. Fill me. Use me.
Spirit of the living God, fall afresh on me.
                           —Daniel Iverson

These are not small changes, minor adjustments we are asking God to make. These are radical, deep changes that happen in us when we enter fully into covenant with God.

Covenant often comes when we are not ready. Covenant often comes where and when we do not want it, and it brings responsibility we would prefer not to take on. But therein lie some of the most risk-filled holy moments we can experience. We may work with people we don't want to be with. We may find ourselves fighting for causes we'd rather leave alone. We may deal with issues we're not quite ready to face.

Covenant with God may mean fighting for the rights of minority persons, working in support of the causes of women, struggling against the military/industrial complex in this country, counseling with those who struggle with the questions of military service. Covenant with God may mean saying no to the use of drugs or alcohol or to loose and irresponsible sex. It may mean not lying or cheating or stealing, not only not stealing someone's goods, but also not stealing another's ideas or writings.

This kind of holy moment may mean we will get dirty, be smelly, and, at times, even get our hair or clothes messed up. It may mean that we will be seen with the poor and outcast, with the radical and revolutionary. It may even mean that we will take up a cross, literally, alone or perhaps with others.

If, therefore, the next few weeks, the next year, the next few years, or even the rest of our lives (as was the case for Moses) seem to be like a wilderness, as we chart a new life, begin a new way, search for new truth, live out a new covenant, we can remember that it is quite all right to be in the wilderness. Some pretty good people have been there before us and are still there with us, folk like Moses, Abraham, Jesus.

It's okay to be in the wilderness, for even there are the certainty and the reality of God's presence for the journey. On their pilgrimage the children of Israel had the symbols of manna, and the pillar of cloud by day, and the pillar of fire by night. We, too, have symbols or signs on our pilgrimage. We have a rainbow that comes in the storm. We still have bread, wine, a towel, and a basin. We have, most of all, a cross.

Yes, covenant with God is risky business indeed. But, ah, what holy moments we do experience living in covenant with God!

Questions for Reflection or Discussion

1. What are some things that entering into covenant with God means to you? Have you entered into any covenants with God? What are they? Would you describe them as *holy*? Why or why not?

2. Is it risky business for you to enter into covenant with God? What are some things that might happen if you enter into covenant with God?

3. What are some symbols, signs of grace, or experiences you have had to sustain you when you have been in your wilderness, after you have entered into covenant and before you have reached the promised goal?

4. Reflect on how the images of baptism, Lord's Supper, and Holy Spirit are covenanting images for you. What commitment has God made in these? What commitment do you make?

5. Talk about some ways entering into covenant with God has gotten some people in trouble through the years. Discuss how entering into covenant with God might get you (your church) into trouble, if you take your covenant seriously.

6.

Seeing

Read Mark 10:46–52

Master, let me receive my sight.
—Mark 10:51b

The story of the healing of blind Bartimaeus in the Gospel of Mark tells of a holy moment. Before Jesus did anything for Bartimaeus, he asked him, ''What do you want me to do for you?'' (Mark 10:51). That seems a little strange as one reads and thinks about that passage. It must have been obvious that Bartimaeus was blind and what he wanted was to be able to see. Jesus had the reputation of helping people and healing people. Surely Bartimaeus wanted Jesus to restore his sight. Anyone should know that.

But the moment becomes holy when we understand that not even Jesus makes assumptions about what our needs are. Jesus wanted to be sure. Too often we in the church think we know precisely what somebody else needs. For far too long, the church has been answering questions no one is asking, prescribing cures for illnesses people do not have, solving problems the world does not have. And in the process of ''knowing,'' we miss the real needs that people have, simply because we do not stop and ask, ''What is it that you really want from God, from the church, or from me?'' Jesus wanted to be sure that he responded to this man's specific felt need at that holy moment. We would do well to remember that Jesus wants us to be specific in stating our needs to him.

The more we reflect on this incident in the life of Jesus, the more we try to understand this passage, the more we may wonder, ''What would I say if Jesus asked me, 'What do you want me to do for you?' '' Stop for just a moment and reflect on that. If you had the opportunity to tell Jesus what you want him to do for you, what would you say?

Perhaps you would respond with one of these statements: ''Give me prestige and status''; ''Give me a nation and a people to rule over''; ''Give me good health''; ''Give me my youth again''; ''Give me a certain person as my lifetime mate''; ''Give me a law degree or a medical degree''; ''Give me a good job with AT&T, GTE, IBM, Burroughs Wellcome, or . . . with just anybody''; ''Give me lots of friends . . . or just *a* friend''; ''Give me my salvation''; ''Give me eternal life''; ''Give me a happy home . . . security in my old age . . . happiness in my youth''; ''Give me good looks, a good singing voice, a good time in life.''

At or near the top of the list may well be the selfsame words Bartimaeus cried out to Jesus, ''Master, let me receive my sight! Master, give me my sight! Give me my sight back! Help me to see, really see, life around me!'' (Mark 10:51, AP). Isn't that one of the most important needs most of us have: to see clearly? Thus, the cry, ''Give me my sight! Restore to me my lost sight! Clarify my vision for me! Give me new sight! Help me to see as you see!'' Seeing is a holy moment.

To think of Bartimaeus as blind, physically unable to see, keeps me from identifying with him, with this story, and keeps Jesus' power seen in this story from really touching me. But when I think of Bartimaeus as not being able to see, not being able to see well or clearly or rightly, or not being able to see as Jesus would have him to see, then there is no way I can keep this story from speaking to me. Blind, I am not. Unseeing, I am.

We may feel a real kinship with Bartimaeus. We may want to say to Jesus at this moment, ''Master, let me receive my sight! Help me see.'' We may want to cry out to Jesus, ''Help me see you; help me see God; help me see others; help me see the world around me; help me see myself.'' A lot of us in this world could know much more of life, life as God intends, if we let Jesus give our sight to us. Seeing is holy. It is a holy moment when we see truly.

A very wise person has said, ''Tragedy is not what we suffer in life, but what we miss.'' We often miss much in life. That's why Bartimaeus' words, when spoken not for those ''blind'' but for those who ''do not see,'' speak for many of us, ''Restore my sight!''

Many of us spend much of our lives seeing things as we want them to be and not as they really are; seeing things that we want to see rather than seeing the accurate picture; seeing things as others tell us they are and not seeing them as they are in reality;

seeing the world through the eyes of others and not seeing the world in the raw, with its breathtaking ugliness and its heart-stopping beauty.

Much of life is spent not seeing. Much of the time we have our eyes wide open, yet we see nothing new or beautiful or repulsive or stimulating or hopeful. How very much of our time are we not seeing? How much of our lives have we spent, are we spending, not seeing? There is so very, very much for us to see and so very, very much that we do not see.

Elizabeth Barrett Browning says it unforgettably in her lines from "Aurora Leigh,"

> Earth's crammed with heaven,
> And every common bush afire with God;
> But only he who sees takes off his shoes—
> The rest sit round it and pluck blackberries.

How many of us go through life "plucking blackberries"? How many of us see "every common bush afire with God"? How many of us see God in our every day? How much of God's world, God's will, God's way, God's people did we see yesterday? Did we see more in our life yesterday than the day before? Were we able to see as we think God wants us to see? Is there more that we want to see, more that God wants us to see?

Certainly there is! There is much more to life for each of us to see than we have seen until now. Jesus saw life as God sees it. Jesus invites us to see life as God sees it, as he, Jesus, sees it. Jesus invites us to the holy moment of seeing.

The point of this story of Jesus and Bartimaeus is

really a very simple one: If we get close to Jesus, if we let Jesus get close to us, if we tell Jesus what we want him to do and have faith in the power and presence of Jesus, life will be different for us. Jesus will change our ways of viewing life.

When we let God touch us, when we become aware that God is touching us, our view is changed, we see differently. We see more clearly.

Jesus can give us new sight in different ways. When we look at Jesus and see his life, who he was, how he lived with others, how he lived with God, what life meant to him, we inevitably see more clearly. We cannot help but see life differently. When we let the eyes of Jesus see through us, see things Jesus wants us to see, see people the way Jesus sees them, see God's world the way Jesus sees it, see ourselves the way Jesus sees us, we cannot help but see differently.

It's that way with our friends. Why shouldn't it be that way with Jesus? When we get close to others or let others get close to us, they change our way of seeing. Let me share some personal experiences to illustrate how this may happen.

A friend I have known many years has a magnificent appreciation of the arts. I love the arts, but I grew up where there were no arts, or at least I didn't know about them. Every time this friend and I are together and he shares some of his feelings about the arts, a painting, a movie, dance, or music, I go away with new sight about the arts.

I have a friend who prays regularly and often, for whom prayer is very important. When she shares with me how beautiful and how meaningful prayer is to her, she transforms my views on prayer.

I have a friend who loves literature. When he talks about poetry or drama or novels, I leave our conversations with my literary sight restored.

I have a friend who is big, dresses casually, and moves slowly. He might not impress you at first. But when he and I talk; when the brilliance of his mind comes through; when I read some of his writings and know how intelligent he is, how much education and learning he has, how the wisdom of the years is in his mind; when he shares all that with me and we part, my view of people who are different from me is changed deeply. To me, my friend is absolutely beautiful! I see more clearly because of him.

A member of my church has changed my view of people in our town. I came here thinking this town was affluent and well-to-do. But as in any other town in this country, some people don't fit into those categories, don't have what I have, don't have what most of us have. This church member has helped me learn about street people and needy people, people who are hungry, lonely, and need a place and need our help. I see other people in a new way because of her.

A growing number of college students today read their Bibles and pray often. When I was an undergraduate, I would not have been caught dead with a Bible in my hands. Now on college campuses students don't mind carrying Bibles, reading them, and praying. One thing these Bible-reading, Bible-carrying, Bible-believing young people have taught me is that if

I am going to be Christian and take the Christian faith seriously, the Bible must be important and central for me. I have learned that all over again. When students tell me what reading and studying the Bible, praying, and talking about the Bible mean to them, my view of the Bible and its importance is transformed. I *see* all over again!

So, if our friends can change our views, and they do it all the time, and restore our sight or give us new sight, how much more can God-in-Christ give us new vision and new sight today. There is no limit to the new vision God-in-Christ can give us. Seeing becomes a holy moment for us.

Once I am able to see, I become responsible. When I get a new insight about what prayer is, or when I learn how significant Bible reading and Bible study is, when I learn about fellow human beings who have needs that I can help to meet, when I get a new vision about any of those things, I become responsible for living out the kind of life God shows I am to live. The blinders are removed, and now I am called to live in God's way.

Jesus says to each of us, "What do you want me to do for you?" If we say in response, "Jesus, give me new sight, restore to me my sight," that is exactly what Jesus will do. If with our heart, soul, and faith, we believe that God-in-Christ can give us new sight and help us see differently, that is exactly what will happen.

Thus, if our plea, our prayer, our word to Jesus is, "Master, restore to me my sight," Jesus will do just that. Jesus *can* make a difference in how we see!

Seeing can become holy for each of us, now and always.

Questions for Reflection or Discussion

1. Have you ever thought of seeing, really being able to see, as being a holy moment or a holy experience? Think for two or three minutes about some moments when your vision has been clarified and you have been made really to see. What was that like?

2. Is it important for us, in relating to Jesus, to be sure we express clearly and specifically what we want Jesus to do for us? How do you seek help from Jesus, more in generalities or more in specifics? If you were telling Jesus the one thing most important that you want him to do for you, what would it be?

3. Reflect upon some ordinary experiences you have had, or you know others have had, that really were afire with God. Share about how you wish you were able to see better or more clearly. What are some aspects of life you wish God would help you see more clearly?

4. In what ways do we become responsible for ourselves and for life around us, once we become able to see? Are there differences between being unseeing and blind? What are they?

5. How would you describe an experience of seeing that was a holy moment for you?

7.

Love

Read 1 John 4:7–11, 19.

Beloved, let us love one another; for love is of God.

—1 John 4:7a

Let me invite you to think about your life just now. What it has been, is, and may be.

Have you ever thought about what life would be like if you had to live all your life with the feeling that no one loved you? Absolutely no one at all?

Have you ever thought about what life would be like if you lived your life, all of it, and you never had the feeling of having loved anyone else? Absolutely no one else at all?

Life would be like hell! I can think of no more descriptive way to think about the agony and emptiness and nothingness of hell than never to have been loved or never to have loved.

In 1 John, the writer is telling us, "You need to be loved to live!" In the Gospel of John, Jesus is telling us, "You need to love to live!" Here is a twofold awareness that love, the love that is for us, is what determines life and the quality of life for each one of us. This twofold awareness of life is beautiful and holy. Love is for us to receive "because [God] first loved us'' (1 John 4:19). Love is for us to give because "greater love has no [one] than this" (John 15:13).

Thus, John and Jesus offer us a two-way experience that is at the heart and soul of life. Moments in which love is given and received are holy moments—the real essence of the abundant life Christ came to bring us. John and Jesus did not, and do not, want us to miss life, nor are we to deny it to others. I wonder what life would be like if we were never loved? What would life be like if we never loved?

Life as many of us live it is not love. Life for many of us is a hellishly lonely, unfriendly, cold, uncaring, cutthroat kind of existence. Ours is a time when many of us do not know what it is, nor how, to receive or give love.

A friend of mine, a young woman with much beauty, intelligence, and ability, wrote me a poignant letter recently, saying, "There is something missing in my life and I am afraid of what may happen to me if I continue on this way. It seems so futile. . . . Life is so lonely. . . . It hurts so much. . . . Please help me."

What is this love we're thinking about—this holy moment? It is not a syrupy, sentimental kind of love. It is not a love that is maudlin or soft and pliable at all.

This love is tough yet gentle, patient yet forthright. It is faithful and enduring, joy-filled and real, serene and secure, kind and caring, good and holy. This holy love means to choose, respond, commit, decide, and risk. This love feels the hurts, needs, and longings of others; sees, really sees and shares the pain, misery, and struggles of others. This love responds to an impulse that is God-initiated and other-directed. This love is that experience which offers not only immediate satisfaction but also ultimate fulfillment. This love is a holy moment.

Love is for us to receive because God first loved us, as John puts it in his first epistle. Thus, God's word shows us that the initiative to love is from God. We believe God loved us uniquely in the coming of Jesus the Christ, in the Incarnation. But God has always been loving. God's love is the personal love of a personal God for persons like you and me. And that is holy. Love is the most important clue to the meaning of God's word and to the gospel of our Lord Jesus Christ: The Bible gives us the old and new love stories between God and us.

The love of God shines through scripture from the story of creation in the Book of Genesis to the final glorious vision of the new Jerusalem on earth in the Book of Revelation. The Old Testament prophets, Jesus, Peter, Paul, John, and other leaders in the early church saw God's love as the basic experience behind every event in their lives and every event they recorded. God's love was so basic that they not only said, "God loves" or "God shows love," but they also said, "God is love." The very nature, character, and essence of God are love. Love is who God is! When God came into human history in the form of the Redeemer, Jesus Christ, it was love in the flesh, divine love in human form. It was a holy moment.

God has been showing us how very much we are loved for a long, long time. God's love for us is seen in the love Miriam had for her brother Moses; the love Joseph had for his brothers and his father; the love Ruth had for her mother-in-law Naomi; the love Jonathan had for his friend David; the love David had for his son Absalom; the love Hosea had for his prostitute-wife Gomer; the love Mary and Elizabeth had for each other; the love Joseph had for his pregnant-out-of-wedlock Mary; the love Andrew had for his brother Peter; the love Peter had for Jesus; the love Jesus has for us. God loves us, which is a beautiful awareness to come to.

Love is for us to give because "greater love has no one than this, that one should lay down one's life for one's friends" (John 15:13, AP). In the Gospel of John, these words come just after Jesus has said, "Love one another as I have loved you" (John 15:12). Again, because God has loved us, we are able to love one another.

Jesus tells us what the ultimate experience, the ultimate expression, the ultimate giving of love would be: to lay down one's life for another. This is love in its ultimate sense. This is love as a holy moment.

If you were looking for someone to be your friend, what kind of friend would you want? One who would care for you just a little, be concerned for a while, think about you briefly, then leave you alone? Or would you want someone who really cared, really was present, really was supportive, really was with you, even to the giving of life itself for you?

Or if you were going to be a friend, what kind of friend would you be willing to be? One who cared for another only when all went well; only as long as the other did not ask for or expect much; only as you could be sure that, for every moment given, every tear shed, every feeling shared, you would get as much or more in return? Or could you, would you, be willing to love all the way, even to laying down your life for another?

Is there anyone, any person you know, any friend you have, for whom you would be willing to lay down your life? Do you know anyone, anyone else on the face of the earth, for whom you would be willing to lay down your life? Is there anyone you know who would be willing to lay down his or her life for you? Anyone at all?

I once thought being loved was the deepest experience one could have, that the greatest joy, the deepest satisfaction, the most complete sense of worth and meaning and wholeness one could know would be the feeling of being loved, totally, freely, and unconditionally. Surely if it is hell never to be loved, it is heaven to know love, feel love, and be loved.

But Jesus says, and this I now believe, that there is a love even greater than being loved. That experience greater than being loved is to love, to love so much, so deeply, so fully, so unconditionally, so unselfishly, so unreservedly that one is willing even to lay down one's life for one's friend. Surely, if it is hell never to love, it is heaven to love, to love another all the way with life, in life, through life, even unto death.

The beauty of God's word is that it tells us we can know both the heaven of being loved, because God first loved us, and the heaven of loving another, for "greater love has no one than this than to lay down one's life for one's friend."

But that's hard, maybe impossible, because few of us will be called on to lay down our lives literally.

Most of us believe we would do that, if the need or opportunity should occur. If we happened upon a burning house, we would probably rush inside and lay down our lives to save a child. If we came across an automobile wreck and the car was about to explode, we would likely rush in to rescue someone trapped inside. If we were at the lake swimming and someone was drowning, we would try, at risk of our own lives, to save that person. Most of us miss the beauty and deep, deep meaning of this magnificent word of Jesus because we think this kind of love comes only when we literally lay down our lives, actually die, for another. But we will not get these kinds of tragic opportunities very often.

I would like to suggest that you have the privilege of laying down your life everyday. Every time you stop and listen and give someone your attention and time, you lay down your life. Every time you reach out to touch and care for another, you give that person some of yourself, your life. Every time you stop and put your arms around someone who hurts or grieves, you give some of your very life to that person. Every time you join in a holy moment of joy or sadness with a friend, and share some time and thought and feeling, you lay down some of your life. Every time you stop to look in the eyes of a child who needs you, or pay attention to an alienated and rebellious youth or young adult, or minister to a couple struggling in their marriage, or spend time with an elderly person, you lay down your life for that friend. That is love given. That is a holy moment. And you and I have this opportunity to lay down our lives all the time.

Lay down your life? Probably not literally. But by the grace of God and for God's sake, for the saving of another and for your sake, you can lay down some of yourself and your time. You can take time to listen, really listen, and give some of yourself for someone. Parent for child. Wife for husband. Husband for wife. Friend for friend. Neighbor for neighbor. Any of us for any other. Just give some of yourself.

Let's look now at the cross of Christ. Here is where and how and when God said, "This is what I mean when I say 'I love you.'" The cross is where and how and when God showed us unforgettably, "Greater love has no one than this." And thus, as we look at the cross, we know about magnificent love, ultimate love. This is ultimate love received and ultimate love given.

The words of the first and last verses of one of our most beautiful hymns—"When I Survey the Wondrous Cross" by Isaac Watts—come to mind:

> When I survey the wondrous cross
> On which the Prince of Glory died,
> My richest gain I count but loss,
> And pour contempt on all my pride.
>
> Were the whole realm of nature mine,
> That were an offering far too small;
> Love so amazing, so divine,
> Demands my soul, my life, my all.

"By this we know love, that Christ laid down his life for us; and we are to lay down our lives for one another" (1 John 3:16, AP).

Let me invite you to think about life just now. Your life. What it has been, is, and is yet to be.

Questions for Reflection or Discussion

1. Reflect upon an experience when you feel you were loved unconditionally; when you were able to show love to another unconditionally. How would you describe your feelings in these two kinds of love—love received and love given?

2. What does it mean to you (or to your church) to lay down your life for your friend? Have you ever? Do you? Would you? How so?

3. Is love, when truly received or given, *always* a holy moment? Does all love come from God? Is love experienced where no one acknowledges or is aware of God's presence?

4. How would you compare your experiences of love received and love given? Which is greater? Why?

5. In what way(s) is the cross a symbol of the supreme holy moment of love we know?

8.

Bad Things

Read 2 Corinthians 1:3–10.

Blessed be the God . . . of all comfort,
who comforts us in all our affliction.
—2 Corinthians 1:3

A question we all ask that is literally as old as Job is, "Why do bad things happen to good people?" Our forebears were asking it before Job; they have certainly been asking it ever since Job's life, experiences, and writings. The question is a simple one; even children ask it. It deals with a common and universal experience in life.

Rabbi Harold S. Kushner has written a book, *When Bad Things Happen to Good People*. It has been widely read and appreciated, for the book deals with this universal question. The book deals with reality, particularly the reality of Rabbi Kushner and his wife. They were living a good and faithful life, yet they experienced the tragedy of their young son's incurable disease. When Aaron was three years old, on the day his younger sister was born, the family pediatrician told them Aaron had progeria, the aging disease. The doctor said Aaron "would never grow much beyond three feet in height, would have no hair on his head or body, would look like a little old man while he was still a child, and would die in his early teens.''

In *When Bad Things Happen to Good People,* Rabbi Kushner writes:

> What I mostly felt that day was a deep, aching sense of unfairness. It didn't make sense. I had been a good person. I had tried to do what was right in the sight of God. More than that, I was living a more religiously committed life than most people I knew, people who had large, healthy families. I believed that I was following God's ways and doing his work. How could this be happening to my family? If God existed, if He was minimally fair, let alone loving and forgiving, how could He do this to me?
>
> And even if I could persuade myself that I deserved this punishment...on what grounds did Aaron have to suffer? He was an innocent child, a happy outgoing three-year-old. Why should he have to suffer physical and psychological pain every day of his life? Why should he have to be stared at, pointed at, wherever he went?...It simply didn't make sense....I could only repeat over and over again in my mind, ''This can't be happening. It is not how the world is supposed to work.'' Tragedies like this were supposed to happen to selfish, dishonest people.... How could it be happening to me, to my son...?

The story is as old as Job. It is as new as last night's fatal automobile accident. It is as far away as the bombed-out homes in Beirut, Lebanon. It is as close as your home or your apartment or as close as the neighbors next door or around the corner. We all know secondhand, and firsthand, what it is to have bad things happen to good people.

Bad things do happen to good people, to very good people. Bad things have always happened to good people. When bad things happen to people, it does not mean the people to whom they happen are bad. Bad things happen to *good people and to bad people*. We have all had bad things happen to us, whether we are good or not. Bad things just happen, to the good and the bad. Good things just happen, to the good and the bad.

Jesus responded to this perplexing reality by saying that the rain falls on the just and the unjust (Matt. 5:45). We know that. The sunshine also falls on the just and the unjust, on the good and the bad. We know that. Kushner reminds us that God has placed us in a world where many more good things than bad things happen to us.

I think that is true. We enjoy more days of health than of sickness. We experience more moments of joy than of sadness. The telephone more often brings good news than bad. The letter more often makes us feel good than bad. Tragedy, pain, suffering, heartache are more the exception than the norm. We have many more sunny days than stormy ones. We meet many more smiles than frowns. It is true that for most of us life is more good than bad. But that does not make the bad any more bearable when it happens.

I want to ask two questions about these experiences common to all of us. First, do bad things happen to good people because this is God's will? I do not think so. The Jews in the Old Testament did not think so. Job did not think so. Jesus did not think so. The early church did not think so. God does not will that the innocent suffer. It is God's will for all persons to know goodness, health, and fulfillment in life. To say that a tragic experience is God's will may seem to help for the moment. But blaming God, saying a bad experience is God's will, may only be the easy way out.

Second, do bad things happen to good people because the suffering one has sinned? Not necessarily so. Jesus clearly refuted this argument. You remember he and his disciples were facing a man blind from his birth. The disciples asked, "Rabbi, who sinned, this man or his parents, that he was born blind?" Jesus answered, "It was not that this man sinned, or his parents" (John 9:2–5).

Some suffering is inevitably the result of sin. But all sin does not result in suffering, and all suffering is certainly not the result of sin.

Why do we think that everything that happens has to have a reason? Why do we think we have to understand everything? Why do we think we have to blame God or others or ourselves when things go wrong or something bad happens? Why can we not simply accept the fact that some things just happen?

It is far more reassuring for me, far more compatible with my view of who God is, far more consistent with the view of God we have in the Old Testament and New Testament and the God we see in Jesus, to have a God who is limited, a God who does not do everything, does not control everything, than to have a God who causes the innocent to suffer, than to have a God who deliberately, willfully causes bad things to happen to good people. Give me a God whose power is limited before you give me a God who capriciously flaunts power and tragedy on the innocent as well as the evil. God *can do anything* and everything God wants to do. I believe that. God chooses not to interfere or intrude into any and all aspects of our life, but chooses to limit, to stand back, to wait, to let us be free and responsible children who will suffer and grow, hurt and heal, fall and fail. All the bad that happens is not because we have sinned.

I am absolutely amazed and appalled at the amount and kinds of suffering some people endure. It is incredible what some people live with, day in and day out. It is unbelievable to know particularly the terrible suffering many children endure and endure bravely and triumphantly.

Bad things do happen to good people. We know that. We have experienced some or many of those bad things ourselves, or our loved ones have. There are no easy answers to explain these experiences common to us all. *Perhaps there are no answers at all!* I hope you can live with that. I hope I can live with that. Namely, that some experiences in life, some bad experiences in life, just happen to good people, and we will not know or find the answers *now.* I think it is far better to have no answers than to have the kind of superficial, nonhelpful talk that Job got from his three "friends." Perhaps Paul was right when he said, "Eye has not seen, nor ear heard, neither has it entered into the heart of anyone, what God has prepared for those who love God" (1 Cor. 2:19, AP).

We have not seen, and we do not know—now. Perhaps Paul was also right when he said, "Now we see in a mirror dimly, but then face to face" (1 Cor. 13:12). We do see dimly. Now. But, one day ...

Perhaps the real question is not, "Do we find answers to the questions of why bad things happen to good people?" Perhaps the important question is the one Kushner poses for us, "What do we do now that bad things have happened to us?" What do you do in the midst of a bad, tragic experience? What do you do when it is over? William James, noted authority on the psychology of religion at the turn of the century, is quoted as saying that the real test of the meaning of any experience is our answer to the question, "What difference does it make?"

I believe we can do three things when bad things happen to good people that will make it possible for these bad things to become holy moments—to have a positive difference in our lives: pray to God; come together with one another; and have faith in God.

We can pray to God. The writer of Lamentations, writing of the laments of the people of Israel over the bad things that had happened to God's good and faithful people, tells us:

> Remember my affliction and my bitterness,
>   the wormwood and the gall!
> My soul continually thinks of it
>   and is bowed down within me.
> But this I call to mind,
>   and therefore I have hope:
> The steadfast love of the Lord never ceases,
>   his mercies never come to an end;
> they are new every morning;
>   great is thy faithfulness.
>
> —Lamentations 3:19–23

One way we know "the steadfast love of the Lord never ceases" is through prayer. Prayer is hard, especially in times of darkness. It may be hard to know God, to find God, to feel God. But sometimes we may have to live with the reality that we do not know God in a given moment and be content that God knows us. We do that in prayer. Prayer in the midst of suffering is a holy moment.

We can come together with one another. Paul tells us in 2 Corinthians that the early Christians in Macedonia had suffered much affliction. Yet, in and through all of that, their love and generosity were examples Paul held up for the church at Corinth and for us. Strange, isn't it, in moments of tragedy, when we hit the bottom rung of life's ladder, when the darkest of clouds hover around and over us, that warm and caring and gentle hands often touch us and hold us up and love us?

One of the things, the beautiful things, about being in church that surprises me and pleases me is to see how much love and affection and attention are focused on a family when some bad thing has happened. Often I think we live a cold, competitive, callous, and uncaring life. And it is much of the time. But when someone hurts or suffers or is in real need, the hard stones become soft hearts, the clenched fists become loving hands, and the preoccupied selves become concerned for others. Tragedy puts us in touch with others. Suffering redeems us from isolation. Bad experiences bring us together in beautiful holy moments. At times in my life the only thing that has kept me going has been the awareness that there is someone who cares. To come together in Christ can make a bad thing a holy moment.

We can have faith in God. Two healing stories in Mark tell us of some good people who had had bad things happen to them. Jairus' daughter was dying, and Jairus was heartbroken. A woman had been suffering with a hemorrhage for twelve years. Bad things. These folk knew them. Do you know what brought healing and health and wholeness, what restored them to new life? Faith. They had faith in Jesus. In the midst of death, heartbreak, and suffering, they simply believed in the power and presence of Christ. They had faith in God.

Sometimes, faith in God is all we can have, and we find the power to endure our suffering. Perhaps that is all we can ever ask for, expect, or hope for—faith in God who will see us through. Faith can transform our suffering into a holy moment.

G. A. Studdert-Kennedy was an Anglican priest, a chaplain in World War I known as "Woodbine Willy." He went through many nightmarish experiences with his comrades in battle. In one of his poems, "Thy Will Be Done", he writes powerfully and movingly in his Cockney accent about our struggle to understand horrible things that happen to us in life. He talks about his friend Bill who left a wife and kiddies at home and was killed in battle. He cannot understand. Then, he remembers our Lord and how our Lord prayed and prayed and yet he had to die. Finally, in unforgettable words, the old Army chaplain reminds us that what came to his friend Bill, what came to God's son Jesus, and what comes to all of us is one thing, real and sustaining: faith in the grace of God which will always see us through.

Sometimes, faith in God is all we can have, and we find the power to endure our suffering. Sometimes, that is all we have. Always, that is enough. Perhaps that is all we can ever ask for, expect, or hope for—faith in God who will see us through. Faith can transform our suffering into a holy moment.

Questions for Reflection or Discussion

1. What is the role of God in bringing about bad experiences in the lives of good people? Does God cause them to happen? Let them happen? Not care if they happen? What do your answers to these questions say about what God is like?

2. Have you ever asked, "How could God do this to me?" What was the situation? Talk about it. Did God do it to you? How so?

3. Can we really believe there is anything holy about many of the bad things we see happening to good or innocent people today? What are some of these bad things? How would you describe them as holy? Or would you describe them as holy?

4. If bad things do not happen as a result of God's will, where is God in all of this and what is God doing?

5. How do we go about accepting the fact that there are some experiences we have, or others have, in life for which there are no answers at all? Can we accept that? Do we want to accept that?

9.

Near Death

Read Psalm 23.

Though I walk through the valley of the
shadow of death, I fear no evil.
　　　　　　　　　　—Psalm 23:4a

Certain experiences in life change us irrevocably.
We are never the same again. When one has walked
near to death; when one has been there, because of a
heart attack, not once or twice but three times; when
one watches one's mother and stepfather die; when
one has surgery on one's vocal cords three times;
when all of this happens—as it has to me in a period
of less than a year—one cannot help but be a changed
person. Being near death is a holy moment.

Life is changed. I see God differently and more
closely. Relationships with my wife have changed. I
see our children in a different light. My friends are
more precious.

All around me is changed. No, I guess that is not
the way it is. I changed most of all, for life is no
more as it was before the first time I walked near
death, and it never will be again.

Now, it is enough just to be. Friends say, "I'm
glad to see you here." I reply, "I'm glad to be here.
As a matter of fact, I'm just glad to be."

Have you ever thought what gratitude should fill our hearts just to be? In *Who Is Man?* Abraham Joshua Heschel reminds us we are to "sense the grandeur of the moment, the marvel and mystery of being, the possibility of quiet exaltation." Just to be is joy and grandeur and exaltation.

But all of that comes to a screeching halt when one walks near death. It is a holy moment to be aware one stands momentarily on the edge between life and death. It is awesome. It is frightening. It is life changing. It is a holy moment.

What was it like to be in the valley near death?

Disconcerting? Yes. For my mind was not long on any single thing or person. I thought far more of persons than of issues or things. I remembered more of "who" than of "what." My mind moved to and fro with no rhyme or reason, and I could neither control this waywardness of mind nor stop it.

Preoccupying? Yes. I had no time for wasted thoughts or feelings. I wanted everything I thought, felt, said, or expressed to be of substance and value to me and to others. My mind was filled with thoughts that simply overflowed like the waters over Niagara. My heart was filled with emotions I had long ago forgotten, or wished I had felt more often, or wished I had shared or could share or would share, or wished I were not feeling then. I was preoccupied, my body was, my mind was, my heart was, with torrents of beauty and mystery I could not have imagined or conceived.

Worrying? Yes. I surely worried. I worried over the past, the present, and mostly over the future. I worried over my body, my mind, my whole self. I asked, "Who am I? What am I? What's going on? Does anybody know? Can anybody help? Will anybody help?" I worried over my wife, my daughters, and my sons. I worried over my job. Job? Oh, yes! Job! (That, above *all* else, I found, went on uninterrupted!) Worry seems natural and inevitable. At least it was for me.

Comforting? Yes. There was peace in the valley when I walked near death. Comfort came from the presence and strength of God's love and grace. Comfort came from friends and family, those whom I hold dear and take for granted; from the cards and notes and expressions of concern; from fruits and flowers and gifts of love and friendship; from phone calls and prayers offered by pastors, neighbors, friends, and family. Comfort came from all the "little things" that aren't so little if you are the one near death.

Never again will I call them *little things*. I even used to think that prayer was one of those little things you did for someone who was sick. That it really did not matter whether or not I prayed when I visited in the hospital. For some, prayer does not matter. For most, and for me now, it makes a big difference. A friend of mine said to me recently, "When you come to see me in the hospital, don't bow your head and say a few words to God up there. Look me straight in the eye and tell me you love me, you care, you will be my friend." I understand what my friend is saying.

I don't want any self-righteous, pious platitudes prayed over me or for me. I surely don't want anyone trying to be certain I'm "saved" when I walk near death. But I do want both: a friend to love me and care for me and look me in the eye and tell me so, and someone who can and will offer genuine prayers of support and intercession for me and my family. Both are holy moments. I want both. I need both. Both work. Both make a difference. A look of love straight in the eye. A prayer of blessing straight from the heart. Both help. I understand now what Henri Nouwen meant when he wrote in *The Wounded Healer,* ''We can survive almost anything in life if we know one person is waiting for us.''

I remember the second heart attack I had. I was out in the middle of the wilds, at a cabin near a lake. It was one o'clock in the morning when the heart pains started. My friend and I started out to find a hospital, and oh, how he cared for me and worried about me. I knew he was with me and would see me through the ordeal.

I knew that many, many miles away, others cared for me and were waiting for me. My wife, my children, and my friends cared and waited. One by one they came to my mind, and I saw them vividly as we drove for almost two hours before finding the hospital. My friends and family, who were waiting for me, kept me alive. I survived, because of them, and yet they never knew how they were saving my life in the dark of night. Sometimes, the caring of another person is enough to keep us going when we walk near death.

I have always been afraid of death and dying, of sick and dying people, and of hospitals and funeral homes. They have always made me nervous and anxious. I am afraid of dying, the experience called ''dying.'' I am afraid of death itself. I am uncertain, and thus afraid, of what is beyond death. But faith helps me. Yet even with faith (and I do have faith in a God who will be with me "always"), I am still afraid.

Ever since I was a little boy and first knew I would die, I have been afraid of death. I was then; I am now. I have preached many sermons on death and dying. Some of them have been pretty good, and some have been helpful to others and to me. I have been with others just before they died; been with some when they died; been with many others, and with their families, just after death occurred. I assure you that this is one dimension of life in which experience does not make it any easier to think about or face death. When I walk with others near death and when I walk near death, I am afraid. Even though I believe in life after death, I am still afraid.

Is that really so unusual or strange, after all? To be afraid of death? I think not. Simply because I like to live, I want to live. I love life. I affirm life. I enjoy life. And, as I understand death, it takes life away from me! I want as much of this life as I can have, as long as I can have it. That is why I'm afraid to die and don't want to die. James Kavanaugh writes, "Death! I despise you!" because death has taken his gentle friend. I'm not sure I despise death. I just don't want to see death come around to my family or friends or me.

As much as anything else that I felt when I walked near death, I felt trusting. When I was told I had experienced my third heart attack, I was ready to hear the doctor say I should have open heart surgery. I told the doctor I was ready for him to do the surgery. As a matter of fact, I was ready after the first heart attack. I felt then, and still do, that I would rather face surgery and take my chances on living or not living than to live in constant fear and dread of what "might" happen. I was ready because I trusted my doctors and nurses. They were experienced, intelligent, skilled, caring, and competent.

I experienced a holy moment when the doctor said, "We need to operate on your heart." The surgery and recovery were filled with many holy moments. As I've heard the procedure described and have seen the looks on the faces of those whom God used to heal me, I have lived through many holy moments.

When one walks near death, life is never the same again. Now, for me, the sun is a little brighter and warmer. Birds sing a sweeter song. The rain falls more softly, and I give thanks for it. The hug of a friend, the clasp of a friend's hand, the look in the eye of one who cares mean more than ever. My mate is no longer presumed upon; I give thanks for her every gesture of love and support and caring. Even the clamor and claims of my children are holy; their expressions of affection and concern and constant presence reach a depth of my soul that is beautiful and unforgettable. When I get out of bed, wash my face, and go for a walk in the yard, I give thanks. My work is no longer "front and center" but takes a new meaning as I put it in its proper perspective. Life has always been good to me and for me. Now, to me, life is not only good, life is holy.

When one walks near death, one appreciates life and living more. The little things in life become big, and many of the big things in life become little. I appreciate those whom God uses in the medical profession to bring healing and wholeness. I have come to know what it takes to heal: others, prayer, love, concern, God's presence, and "the unknowns" of life. I have learned a newer and deeper sympathy for others who are in the hospital or are confined at home.

Most of all, I have a new appreciation of life. I want to live—and live life all the way! As Carl Sandburg said in his poem "High Moments":

I have kept high moments.
They go round and round in me.

When once you have walked near death, life is never the same. Life itself is one grand and glorious high moment—holy moment—that does indeed go round and round in you. Thank God!

Questions for Reflection or Discussion

1. Have you ever had an experience when you thought you were going to die? Share some of your feelings you recall. Has your life been different since that experience?

2. What are some thoughts and feelings you might have if you were going through an experience that could mean your death? Talk with another (the group) about your feelings. What are some priorities of your life that you might reorder if you knew death was near for you?

3. If you were critically ill in the hospital, what kind of visitors would you like to have? What would

you like for people to talk about with you? In your presence? Do you want your pastor to pray with you, for you, when he or she visits you in the hospital? Why? What would you like him or her to pray for?

4. ''When one walks near death, life is never the same again.'' Do you believe this is true? If you answer yes, and if the changes are mostly for the better, why do you think it takes a near-death experience for us to live as we should be living all along?

10.

Loss through Death

Read Revelation 21:1–5.

[God] will wipe away every tear from their eyes, and death shall be no more.
—Revelation 21:4a

In his book, *Good Grief,* Granger Westberg describes seven responses we have to any serious, personal loss—loss of a job, a home, good health, an arm or leg or the ability to walk or move, sight, the impending loss of life through death, or the loss of a loved one through death. These responses are denial, emotional outbursts, physical distress, anger, guilt, loneliness or withdrawal, and readjustment to the reality of painful change in one's life. Westberg's insightful book is one of the few writings that deals with loss from both the theological and the psychological perspectives.

When we consider that loss through death is one of those holy-moment experiences for all of us, it is helpful to let God's word speak to us about life and death, about hope and promise, about the reality of loss and the assurance of God's grace in and beyond our loss. In John 11, Jesus' experience with the death of Lazarus offers two clear, simple insights that guide us in our losses. God's word says we may grieve.

God's word says that, beyond our grief, we are to live again.

In some instances death brings relief from suffering and misery, from hopelessness and despair. In such experiences, death seems to be better than life. In those moments and on those occasions, death may be good. Ordinarily, we do not welcome death. Death is the human, physical end of life. Loss through death is tragic; it hurts. There is a finality about death that we come to know and acknowledge that is fearful.

In the plan of creation, our God did not intend death. God's divine plan and intention had been for life. Death was not God's gift in the Garden of Eden. Life was. Death was not God's gift in the incarnation of Christ. Life was, the abundant life we find in and through Jesus the Christ. Death was not what God offered in the resurrection of Jesus from the grave. In the resurrection the love and grace of God did not succumb to death, did not honor death, did not call death "good." God in Christ triumphed over death. "The last enemy . . . death" (1 Cor. 15:26) was (and is) conquered and overcome.

It is important to acknowledge death as the enemy so we can counter what Elie Wiesel says he often sees in the Christian faith. Wiesel, in *Harry James Cargas in Conversation with Elie Wiesel*, talks about how "Christians sanctified death." In many of our Christian writings and preachings, we do tend to sanctify death. Often, we make death into something good or beautiful, perhaps even holy.

Death is not the will of God in scripture. Death is reality, loss, pain, hurt, emptiness, mystery, sometimes inexplicable. It is good to claim death and name it that, but let's not call it "God's will"! The experience of loss through death can be a holy moment for us, but Paul calls it "the enemy." Death destroys. It takes away. It brings loss.

Because death is a painful holy moment, filled with loss, God's word tells us we may grieve. "Jesus wept" (John 11:35). How real. How human. How honest. "Jesus wept." That means it is okay for us to cry, to grieve, to weep. It is not only okay, it is absolutely necessary. We need very much to understand and believe that. It is okay for us to grieve when death takes a loved one. It is okay for all of us, men and women, to cry. We are all free to express our grief, set free by the example of Jesus.

John does not write that Jesus was strong; that he accepted Lazarus's death as God's will; that he was brave. No, John said, "Jesus wept." His friend had died. Jesus hurt. He cried. He grieved.

Why do we put an extra burden on ourselves and others, at the time of death, to try to pretend that nothing has happened? When we love someone, death brings a holy moment of loss and grief. Sorrow is inevitable, and it is essential for us to express our sorrow.

There are experiences and moments after loss through death when our days are heavy; when nothing and no one is able to warm us or help us; when life seems cold and cruel; when we feel all alone and know only emptiness and heartache. Sorrow has come, is real, and must be expressed. "Jesus wept." We can be glad he did.

Michel Quoist writes in his book *Prayers*:

Lord, it is dark.
Lord, are you here in my darkness?
Your light has gone out....

. . . .
I should like to leave,
Run away,
Flee,
Anywhere, escape.
Escape what?
You, Lord, others, myself, I don't know,
But leave,
Flee....

. . . .
Lord, it is dark.
Lord, are you here in my darkness?
Where are you, Lord?
Do you love me still?
Or have I wearied you?
Lord, answer,
Answer!

It is dark. Sometimes when it is dark, we cry out, even as our Lord, "My God, my God, why hast thou forsaken me?" Sorrow is great, We grieve.

But just as surely as we are to grieve, we are to live again. Jesus did not stay at the grave of Lazarus. Neither did David linger over the death of his child.

The story of David and the death of his child is one of the most touching, tender, and memorable stories ever written and one most helpful for us. David's child was sick, critically ill, near the moment of death. While the child was struggling between life and death, David prayed, fasted, prostrated himself on the ground, and pleaded with God on behalf of the child. He was so obsessed with praying, fasting, and pleading that the elders of the house tried to get him up and could not.

Then the child died.

David had been so distraught over the child's illness that the elders were afraid to tell him the child had died, afraid that he might harm himself or do something else unpredictable. The elders told him, "He is dead." David's response surprised the elders. His response was not what we would expect either. The scriptures tell the rest of the story in a beautiful way.

> Then David arose from the earth, and washed, and anointed himself, and changed his clothes; and he went into the house of the Lord, and worshiped; he then went to his own house; and when he asked, they set food before him, and he ate. Then his servants said to him, "What is this thing that you have done? You fasted and wept for the child while it was alive; but when the child died, you arose and ate food." He said, "While the child was still alive, I fasted and wept; for I said, 'Who knows whether the Lord will be gracious to me, that the child may live?' But now he is dead; why should I fast? Can I bring him back again? I shall go to him, but he shall not return to me."
> —2 Samuel 12:20–23

As long as there is life or hope, we yearn and pray and plead and lay our souls bare to bring back, to recover, or to continue life for one whom we love. David demonstrated this movingly. But once his child had died, David knew that suffering though he was

91

from the loss of his son, he must live again. Life must go on. Not just stoically or bitterly or resignedly. But we must live again, honestly, realistically, and fully.

In this experience of learning to live again, we come to know that healing is a mysterious and beautiful process initiated by God and carried on by others. We live again, as we let others touch us, help us, care for us. In her book *Death: The Final Stage of Growth*, Dr. Elisabeth Kübler-Ross gently and helpfully says that as others reach out, "it takes so little effort to make such a big difference." "It takes one human being who really cares to make a difference between life and death." To make our loss a holy moment.

We live again when we accept and believe God's word in the Twenty-third Psalm:

> The Lord is my shepherd; I shall not want.
>> He maketh me to lie down in green pastures:
>> he leadeth me beside the still waters.
>> He restoreth my soul: he leadeth me in the
>> paths of righteousness for his name's sake.
>> Yea, though I walk through the valley of the
>> shadow of death, I will fear no evil: for
>> thou art with me; thy rod and thy staff
>> they comfort me.
>> Thou preparest a table before me in the pres-
>> ence of mine enemies: thou anointest my
>> head with oil; my cup runneth over.
>> Surely goodness and mercy shall follow me
>> all the days of my life: and I will dwell
>> in the house of the Lord for ever.
>> —Psalm 23, KJV

Questions for Reflection or Discussion

1. Is death frightening to you? Reflect for two or three minutes on how you feel about death. Share some of your feelings with another person (the group).

2. Is death the only loss that brings us grief? Think about other losses you have experienced over which you have grieved. Look at the responses Westberg says we have to loss and see with which of these you identify. How can we help one another to move to the last two stages?

3. Can you recall some experiences when death has been good? Think about them. What made death good or desirable in those instances?

4. In what way(s) do you believe death was a part of God's divine plan for human beings? In what way(s) was it not? Is death God's will? Talk about your beliefs on this and share differences of belief on this with another person (the group).

5. John writes that Jesus wept. What does that tell us about Jesus? About ourselves? About how we may feel over the death of a loved one?

11.

Leaving

Read Exodus 6:2–8; 13:17–24.

*I will take you for my people, and I
will be your God.*

—Exodus 6:7

For many of us, the word *Exodus* symbolizes the
story of deliverance for the children of Israel from
bondage to liberation, from slavery to freedom, from
brokenness to wholeness, from no people to God's
people. It is the story of a people who were oppressed,
enslaved, trapped, until God's presence and power
came to set them free. It is the story of how leaving
can be a holy moment. This story of the Israelites'
deliverance is found in Exodus, Leviticus, and Numbers.

The Exodus tells us what it is to struggle: pain,
loneliness, weariness, deprivation, disappointment, idola-
try, unfaithfulness/faithfulness, anger, resentment,
looking back, war, famine, second-guessing of them-
selves, Moses, and God.

The Exodus tells us what it is to live searching:
wandering, journeying, believing, doubting, leaving
behind, taking risks, trusting the future, moving.

The Exodus tells us what it is to be in pilgrimage: from Egypt to Canaan, from the Red Sea to the

Jordan River, from slavery to freedom, from Moses to Joshua, from no people to God's people.

Exodus is leaving with no certainty. It is, as someone aptly put it, to exchange "some bad certainties for some good uncertainties." That's not how most of us live. Most of us would rather hold on to the certain and sure, even if it is bad or not helpful, than move toward some potentially good uncertainties. Exodus is living with the likelihood that our plans, our futures, our very lives, will surely change. Exodus means leaving, and leaving is a holy moment, a moment of change for this time, for now, for everyone.

Leaving means believing God. It means to appropriate and live by God's word. Listen to this word, some three thousand years old, yet real for us today: "I will be your God. I am the Lord . . . I will bring you out . . . I will deliver you . . . I will redeem you . . . I will take you for my people . . . I will be your God . . . I will bring you into the land . . . I will give it to you . . . I am the Lord" (Exod. 6). Here is a word worthy of our total trust, a word fit to support any leaving we ever have to do.

As we reflect on the holy nature of leaving, we discern three stages in a leaving experience: having motivation to leave, entering into an agreement, and persevering until the promise is received. Thus, a fitting question at any point in one's life, at any moment, is, "Why should I change? Why should I leave or alter my life?" There must be motivation to leave or change or else we stay as we have been, in the same place physically, mentally, and spiritually.

Robert Kemper writes in *An Elephant's Ballet*, "I am willing to risk new ventures if I think the old ones have not been good enough." Many of us today are looking for some new ventures, new direction, new goals for investing ourselves and our energies. I understand how many people feel as they think about the meaning of the Exodus story for their lives: many feel they have been in bondage; have been subject to the laws and edicts of society or family or "others"; have suffered, been oppressed, mistreated, misunderstood, unappreciated. Now some want to leave that all behind and be on their way. They may not have reached their promised land. Indeed, few have! But they want to take a step in that direction. As we leave, we want to know we are headed for the land of Canaan.

Some of us think a change in scenery will help. "Nothing can be worse than where I am. Anything will be better than what I have now. Oh, if I can only get away from here." Where we are now or where we will be will never be any better than where we have been, unless there are changes other than in the scenery. A change in residence alone will not improve our lot in life. It takes more.

Leaving begins when we know something about where we are going. Leaving is not just denying the past. If all we do is deny the past, our movement will be negative and fruitless. If we accept and affirm the future, we are free then to deny the past in a healthy and positive way. Holy leaving takes place when we see the new as promise. Exodus for the children of Israel began when Moses came away from the burning bush, where he had heard God's voice, and then was able to tell his people and Pharaoh something about where they were going.

Holy leaving is not only going from, it is going toward! The late Dr. Georgia Harkness, a great United Methodist theologian, who died when she was well into her eighties, is quoted as saying, "Be careful what you set your heart on, for you will surely get it!" Leaving requires, first, motivation. Let us be careful what our motivation is. Be sure it points to the future and doesn't just condemn the past.

Here, again, we encounter covenant as a holy moment. Holy leaving involves the taking of a covenant: "I will be your God . . . you shall be my people." Perhaps it would be helpful, as we think of personal and corporate leavings, for us to consider entering into a new covenant with God and a new covenant with those around us.

Covenant with God. William James once said, "Our belief at the beginning of a doubtful undertaking is the one thing that assures the successful outcome of our venture." Leaving is often traumatic. That is why covenant with God is reassuring and helpful. In the book *The Little Prince* by Antoine de Saint-Exupery, the Little Prince tells the Fox, "That which is essential is invisible." So it is with covenant with God: essential and invisible. We can't see it. We can't handle it. We can't measure it or put our arms around it. But there are times this "essential, invisible" covenant is the one, the only thing, that upholds and sustains us.

Covenant with God does not guarantee anything. Covenant does not guarantee faithfulness on the part of the people. Covenant does not guarantee that all will go well with the people. Covenant does mean that God is present to us, that we are present to God; that, if we are faithful to God, God will be faithful to us and will fulfill the promises made to us. "I will be your God . . . I will deliver you." The Exodus experience of the children of Israel kept them in the wilderness forty years. Forty years is a long, long time to wander and search and struggle just to stay alive.

The wilderness is where the people felt lost, where they rebelled, where they pleaded for Moses to take them back, where they built golden calves for idols, where they grew bitter toward one another and angry toward God. The wilderness is also the place where they repented, where they came to their senses, where they remembered their covenant and commitment, where they built the ark as a symbol for worship and as a constant reminder of God's presence with them. Covenant with God assures us only of God's presence in our wilderness.

Covenant with those around us. We need those around us. Those around us need us. Most of us put up a good front most of the time, a front that says, "I'm independent. I can get along quite well by myself." Yet deep, deep inside, what we want to say is, "Why doesn't someone break through? Why doesn't someone reach out? Why doesn't someone touch me or care for me?"

Surely there were times during the Exodus when the Israelites were sustained only by the common bond, the covenant, they had with one another. It's like the story of the little girl who went to the store for her mother. She was gone a rather long time and when she returned, her mother asked why it had taken her so long. She told her mother about another little girl who had fallen and broken her doll and that she had helped her. The mother wondered what she could have done to help the little girl fix her broken doll. She replied, "I just sat down and helped her cry." Covenant means that sometimes we just sit down and help each other cry.

There is another word about covenant with one another. Persons who enter into covenant with one another do not intentionally or willfully hurt one another. There are times, as we go through life, when we do hurt one another. It's inevitable. Please, in Christ's name, let us not willfully hurt or demean any other person. If hurt comes, let it be by accident. And then if it comes, ask for forgiveness at once. Do not let a hurt linger.

On the other side of this coin, we need to be very careful about who we let hurt us. Yes, that's right. Be careful who we let hurt us! Some people have the right to hurt us in love and for our own good. But there are others who do not have that right. That some people do not have the right to hurt us is seen in a line in the movie *Heaven Can Wait*. Julie Christie is put down by Dyan Cannon. Cannon tries to soften her harsh words by saying, "I don't mean to hurt you." Christie replies with real insight and strength, "Oh, that's all right. You don't know me well enough to hurt me." It is important for us to try not to let hurt come to us from those who don't know us well enough to hurt us.

Leaving means persevering until we receive the promise. Persevere a long time, even forty years. The promise of God is the same to us as to the children of Israel, for sustenance, for direction, and for destination. The sustenance is manna, gathered every day by the wandering nomads in the desert. The direction is by way of a pillar of cloud by day and a pillar of fire by night. The destination is "a land flowing with milk and honey." In our leaving, the promises of God are ours if we persevere, if we keep the covenant and remain faithful and obedient along the way.

We do, however, have a part to play in making our leaving holy. God issues the call; God makes the promise; God offers the covenant. God tells us the story of our going out. We listen. We tell one another. We discover holy moments as we make our way. We respond. We are receptive and willing to be led. We are eager recipients, yet willing to be active and involved. It's like a paperweight my daughter gave me. The words on it read, "Pray to God . . . but keep rowing to shore." We pray to God. We remember the covenant. We persevere until the promise comes. After a long and very difficult course one semester in divinity school, the professor began the last lecture by quoting from Matthew, "[the one] who endures to the end will be saved" (10:22).

In our leaving which we may experience in the here and now, or at anytime along the way, there is a word for each of us who enters into covenant with God. One of the things that has sustained those who have gone before us and that sustains us is remembering that God loves us. In our leaving, our going out and our coming in, from this time and forevermore, let us remember always that God is loving us.

Questions for Reflection or Discussion

1. Reflect on some exodus experience when you left the familiar to move to the unknown. What were/ are some of your feelings? Think about the exodus or leaving of someone else from you. How did/do you feel about that leaving?

2. What are some feelings that are quite natural for us to have when we pack up and move on, when we risk new ventures? Does God's grace become more or less present and active in a leaving and going forth?

3. What are some symbols or acts or gestures that have sustained you when you have been in an exodus experience—a phone call, a letter, a visit from someone in the place you have moved to or from? What are some thoughts, feelings, experiences, places, or people you would like to leave behind you? How can you go about leaving the past in the past?

4. In what ways does leaving take faith? Can we venture out, in risk, without faith? How does God help us, sustain us, in our leaving, our going, our arriving?

5. "Leaving means persevering until we receive the promise." Reflect on that statement. How do we find strength to persevere in difficult times, in our "wilderness"? "Those who endure to the end, the same shall be saved." Do you find this statement helpful or not helpful? Why?

12.

Resurrections

Read Matthew 28:1–10.

Do not be afraid; for I know that you seek Jesus who was crucified. He is not here; for he has risen, as he said.
—Matthew 28:5–6

A friend wrote recently, "There is no one, who at one time or another, has not been raised from the dead. The only problem is that most of us do not recognize resurrection when it comes to us." I believe that. I know that. I read that in the scriptures. That is the message of life all around us, as we see it, know it, and experience it. That is the story of the Old Testament and the New Testament. Resurrection. Life—new, good, and holy—happens to us. It happened to Jesus. It happens all the time.

On Easter, we celebrate that what seems to be true is true. What is too good to be true, in fact, is true. What our Lord promised as true has become true. What Jesus assures us is true is true. That truth is that all of God's children can know life because resurrection happens and it happens all the time.

One problem we have in looking at the life of Jesus is that we tend to think crucifixion/resurrection experiences come only at the end of Jesus' life. In looking at our own lives we think crucifixion/resurrection experiences come only at the end of our lives, when we die and are resurrected. But the truth is that both crucifixion *and* resurrection experiences happen to us as they did to Jesus. They happen to us all along the way of life. Our task, then, is to see the life of Jesus whole, and to see those crucifixion/resurrection experiences that happened to Jesus along the way. We also are to see our own lives whole, and to see the crucifixion/resurrection experiences that happen to us all along the way as a part of the whole of life.

Mary said, "I have seen the Lord" (John 20:18). Paul wrote, "[Christ] appeared also to me" (1 Cor. 15:8). When we think about it, these are rather presumptuous, perhaps even arrogant, boasts for Mary and Paul to make. There were probably lots of others in Jerusalem who claimed that Jesus had appeared to them. I have tried, very hard as a matter of fact, to imagine what it would have been like to have been among the people to whom Jesus appeared after he was dead, was placed in the grave, and was raised. When we try to imagine ourselves among those to whom Jesus appeared, we find it hard to fathom the impact Jesus must have had on them when he appeared to them.

Some lines in the movie, *The Last Picture Show,* help us see the meaning Jesus has for us today. These same words help me see the impact Jesus had on the people to whom he appeared. Robert A. Raines, in his book *To Kiss the Joy,* writes about *The Last Picture Show:*

> [Christ] appeared also to me in a movie called
> *The Last Picture Show,* a poignant view of life

in a small Texas town. The town is boring. People feel as though their options are closing off. They yearn for something or someone more. There is much human unfulfillment in the movie, but also little oases of human warmth and understanding. A middle-aged woman talks to a young man about a man they both loved called Sam the Lion. Sam had died. He was a generous, compassionate, and courageous man. The woman had been married to someone else, but she loved Sam in a special way. She said to this young man, ''You know, it's a shame to meet only one man in your life who knows what you are worth.''

Mary, Thomas, John, Peter, and many, many others all had met Someone who knew exactly what each of them was worth. We can meet that Someone, face-to-face. And when we do, that is a holy moment!

Camus, the existentialist playwright, is quoted as saying, ''At the center of life, dominating the great moments of our lives, there is an essential absurdity.'' At the great moments of our lives, what we experience really is an essential absurdity. Sure, resurrection is absurd! Absolutely absurd! But it is an essential absurdity. An early church writer also professed, ''I believe. I believe because it is absurd.'' It really is. It is absurd for the risen Christ to have appeared to Paul or Mary. It is absurd for the risen Christ to appear to any of God's children through history. It does not make sense. There is no way to understand or make sense out of the living presence of Christ. Except, maybe, God-in-Christ really does know how much each one of us is worth. And so, it is absurd. We may choose to believe it is more than that. It is absurdity transformed. Transformed into experience. Transformed into reality we can know. Transformed into a living, ongoing, sustaining experience with God-in-Christ.

If we were to ask, "How many of us have ever had a resurrection experience?" what would be our response? Have you ever had a resurrection experience? If you have, how do you describe it? What has it been like? Would you want to experience the presence of the risen Christ? If you want that, if you expect that, what do you think it would be like? Resurrection experiences with Christ do happen and they happen today, all the time. They happen in different ways to different people, in different circumstances; for different reasons; with different expectations; and with different results. Yes, resurrection happens all the time. When resurrection happens, it is always a holy moment.

The resurrection experiences of Jesus were different, as his resurrection appearances are described for us in the New Testament. There were two men walking down the road to Emmaus. They didn't recognize Jesus. They stopped to eat bread together. In the breaking of the bread and the sharing of the meal, Jesus became known to them.

Thomas the doubtor was in the upper room. He said the only way he would believe would be to put his finger into the side of Jesus. There they were, some friends gathered together to talk, to reminisce, and to share, and Jesus appeared to them.

Mary was visiting a grave, the grave of her friend, one who had cared for her, one who had given her a sense of worth and meaning. He had done all in his physical life that he could do for her. But she had some things more that she was going to do for him. Jesus came to her.

Saul was on the road to Damascus. He was going not to preach Christ but to persecute Christ and the early Christians. As Saul walked along, Jesus appeared to him.

A look at the experiences that these people had with the risen Christ says unequivocally and unquestionably that there is no one place, no one way, no one time, no predictable occasion for us to experience the power and presence of the risen Christ. We may be up or down; happy or sad; believing or doubting; critic or enemy; friend or stranger; ready or not ready. The power and presence of the risen Christ do indeed appear to us, in those serendipitous holy moments of life.

Three things about these experiences are worth noting. First, all of these experiences happened when people were doing routine, ordinary kinds of things, such as eating a meal, walking down the road, gathering with friends in a room, going to a grave. The presence of Christ is in ordinary, simple things that we do every day. Second, none of these people expected Christ to appear to them. It was unexpected for each of them, and it may be unexpected for us. Third, Christ's appearances were not spectacular or overwhelming. As a matter of fact, Jesus tried to downplay them. He simply said, "Peace be with you . . . peace be with you."

Many of us think that in order to know and experience the presence of Christ, something dramatic or overpowering must occur. That is not the truth. The real miracle of the coming of Jesus, in his birth, life, death, and resurrection, is that he came to live with us, in us, among us, where we are and just as we are. He came to be with us in the simple beauty and the hard reality of life as each of us lives it every day.

It is unfortunate that we have romanticized and glamorized the resurrection appearances of Christ. When we do, it is our loss, and a great loss it is. Many are the times that we wish we could recognize, and thus experience, resurrection where God intended, namely, in the commonplace and the everyday. I recently heard a powerful word of warning, "Beware of anyone whose God is in heaven." God may be in heaven, but the cross and resurrection tell us that if God is in heaven, God is also *right here with us in the here and now!*

We have all experienced resurrection appearances of Jesus, because they happen all the time. Perhaps it happened to you the first time you loved. Or when you were sixteen, asserted your independence, and began to get a sense of what it is to be a person in your own right. Or when you went away to college or to work and others did not know about your background or your grades or your accomplishments, and they accepted you and loved you just as you were without any credentials. Perhaps it happened when you were first married, or when your first child was born. Or when you and your spouse had a hard time, and in the midst of that struggle, love came back again and brought new life to you. Resurrection may have happened when you were divorced and then started life over again. Perhaps resurrection happened to you when you confronted the inevitability of your death and found reassurance from God in the midst of that confrontation.

By overdramatizing the experiences of Christ as he appeared to the early church we have glorified resurrection and made it something out of the ordinary. Thus, we have taken Christ out of the everyday world in which we live. How beautiful it would be to read again the resurrection stories, clear away all the dramatics we have added, and experience resurrection in the here and now.

That happened for me while I was in the hospital with my first heart attack. I had a telephone call one evening from a pastor friend in Chicago. He explained that he was on his way to a prayer meeting in his church. Then he went on, ''I am sorry to hear that you are ill. I just wanted to call to read a passage of scripture with you, to pray, and to let you know that our entire congregation is going to be praying for you in a few minutes.'' He read some verses from Psalm 119 and prayed for me. Then, resurrection happened to me!

It is true and verifiable that resurrection experiences happened not only to Jesus or to those in the early church. Resurrection experiences happen to us all the time. It may be somebody's touch. It may be a look that someone gives you to tell you that you are worth something. It may be somebody giving you an assuring word that helps you hold on just a little longer. It may be that hungry child who is being fed. It may be some walls of hatred being broken down or some walls of racism being shattered. It may be the sounds of war growing silent. It may be somebody who simply puts his or her arm around you. Resurrections like these are always holy moments.

There is a legend that tells of a particular kind of bird that has only one song to sing in its whole life. It looks for a bush, a thorn bush, before it sings that song. And once it has found the bush, the thorn bird sings such a glorious and beautiful song that all the earth stands still to listen. Even God in heaven smiles as the bird sings. Then the thorn bird impales itself on the longest of all the thorns on the bush and dies. That story makes good reading, but that is not the gospel! The gospel says that we have not just one song to sing. We have many songs to sing. We sing them over and over and over and over, every time we experience resurrection. Yes, there is Someone who knows how very much each of us is worth. God knows. And God wants us to sing songs all our lives, when holy moments, resurrection experiences, happen to us all along the way.

Questions for Reflection or Discussion

1. Can you recall some resurrection experience(s) in your life? Think about it/them for three or four minutes. What happened? Will you share some of what your resurrection experience(s) meant and mean to you?

2. Do you think there is someone else who knows what you are really worth? Is it really important for us to feel that someone else knows what we are worth? Why?

3. How do you think we experience the resurrection presence of Christ today? How do you? How do

you think others do? Is it always a "spiritual" experience? What kind of experience is it? Can/ does the Christ appear to us in the commonplace experiences of life, or just in the big, "religious" moments?

4. What difference do you think it would make to you (or to others) to believe that the Christ could/ does appear to us in the ordinary? Would that change your/our faith? Our expectations from life? How so?

5. "We have romanticized...the resurrection appearances of Christ." Do you think this is true? How or how not? Do you really feel Christ is *with* you, *near* you, *in* you? Share how this is or is not true for you. How many "songs" about resurrection experiences do you have to sing? Where and how do you sing them?

Dr. Robert T. Young, senior minister of the Broad Street United Methodist Church in Statesville, North Carolina, received the A.B. degree in religion from the University of North Carolina at Chapel Hill; the M.Div. degree from the Divinity School of Duke University, Durham; and was awarded an honorary D.D. degree from Pfeiffer College, Misenheimer, North Carolina. He has also studied for a year with William Barclay at the University of Glasgow, Glasgow, Scotland.

Prior to his ministry at Broad Street United Methodist Church, Dr. Young served as Dean of the Chapel and Minister to the University at Duke University for ten years. He has also served pastorates in North Carolina and Scotland.

Noted and in demand as a preacher, teacher for Schools of Christian Mission, and a spiritual life retreat leader, Dr. Young has written articles for many outstanding journals and periodicals. An earlier book, *A Sprig of Hope,* was published by Abingdon Press.

Dr. Young and his wife live in Statesville, North Carolina. They are parents of two daughters and two sons.